RURAL COMMUNITY DECLINE
AND REVITALIZATION

GARLAND REFERENCE LIBRARY
OF SOCIAL SCIENCE
(Vol. 443)

RURAL COMMUNITY DECLINE
AND REVITALIZATION
An Annotated Bibliography

Brenda L. Ekstrom
and
F. Larry Leistritz

GARLAND PUBLISHING, INC. • NEW YORK & LONDON
1988

Library of Congress Cataloging-in-Publication Data

Ekstrom, Brenda L.
Rural community decline and revitalization : an annotated
bibliography / Brenda L. Ekstrom and F. Larry Leistritz.

p. cm.—(Garland reference library of social science; v.
443)
Bibliography: p.
Includes indexes.
ISBN 0–8240–2433–8
1. Rural development—Bibliography.   2. Rural development—United
States—Bibliography.   3. Rural conditions—Bibliography.   4. United
States—Rural conditions– Bibliography.   5. Regional planning—
Bibliography.   6. Regional planning—United States—Bibliography.
I. Leistritz, F. Larry.   II. Title.   III. Series.

Z7164.C842E4   1988   [HN49.C6]   016.3071′4—dc19
88–2418   CIP

Printed on acid-free, 250-year-life paper
Manufactured in the United States of America

Contents

Acknowledgments

Writing the acknowledgments is always a pleasure because it offers us an opportunity to thank our colleagues who participated in creating this bibliography. First, we want to thank Susan Bartuska who typed many of the annotations and was always willing to meet our deadlines. Her cooperation and help is greatly appreciated.

We extend our appreciation to the North Central Regional Center for Rural Development at Ames, Iowa, for providing funds in support of our efforts, which should benefit researchers in the agriculturally dependent North Central region as they work to understand the current economic crisis and strive to revitalize rural communities. Our thanks also go to Dr. Peter F. Korsching, Director of the center, for his continued support and encouragement.

Our appreciation is also extended to Deb Sayler, Lorrettax Mindt, and Marcia Smoyer of the Interlibrary Loan system at North Dakota State University (NDSU). Their ability and willingness to secure hundreds of works for us in a very timely manner permitted us to complete this bibliography in a relatively short period of time. Without their help and the cooperation of other libraries we could not have produced such an extensive and complete book. We also thank Kathy Hollenhorst of the NDSU library for conducting the computer searches for us. Her skills in narrowing our topics were greatly appreciated.

In addition, we acknowledge the support of the Department of Agricultural Economics at NDSU, the useful reviews of Tim Mortensen and Dean Bangsund of that department, and the many researchers throughout the United States who responded to our request for books, articles, and reports to include in this bibliography. Their assistance made it possible for us to include many current works that have not yet appeared in professional journals, indexes, and computer data bases.

As always, our gratefulness to these individuals and entities does not implicate them for any remaining errors or omissions.

Introduction

Many areas of rural America have experienced a substantial reversal of fortunes during the 1980s. The previous decade had been a period of economic and population growth for most rural areas, but the 1980s have seen rural growth rates slip substantially behind those of metropolitan areas. In fact, preliminary information now indicates that the much-touted migration turnaround of the 1970s (a term many demographers used to denote the reversal of the historic pattern of net migration from nonmetropolitan to metropolitan counties) has reversed in the 1980s.

Rural areas dependent on such resource-based industries as agriculture, mining, and forestry have been particularly hard-hit. In addition, some manufacturing industries, which were attracted to rural areas by low labor and operating costs, are now increasingly relocating abroad, where such costs are even lower.

Reductions in the output and employment of a dominant industry can have a myriad of effects on local communities. Immediate loss of jobs and income may stimulate some persons to leave the area in search of better opportunities. A significant loss of human resources through outmigration can seriously impair the ability of a community to mobilize its residents and resources to address its problems. Faced with declining income and population in their trade areas, local retail businesses and service firms may be forced to make severe adjustments, and local governments may find it difficult to remain solvent and to maintain services.

Social effects also occur in an economically declining area. The sense of despair and helplessness felt by many individuals and families as they experience the loss of their livelihood and social ties has become prevalent. Continuing economic decline and outmigration can lead to a degradation of the overall social and institutional fabric of a community.

The problems associated with economic decline are now being confronted by much of rural America, and a new awakening of interest in rural development, or as it has increasingly been termed *rural revitalization*, is occurring. The rekindled interest in the economic revitalization of rural communities might at first appear to be merely a reincarnation of the rural development movement of the 1960s and early 1970s, but a

number of new emphases have appeared in the last few years:
(1) greater attention to retaining and expanding existing
firms, rather than merely to attracting new industry; (2)
heightened interest in the process by which new enterprises
are created, commonly referred to as *entrepreneurship*; (3)
growing recognition that some communities may be able to
strengthen their economic bases through such relatively
nontraditional means as attracting service sector activities
(e.g., medical facilities), which serve clientele extending
beyond the local area; and (4) recognition of the changing
roles of various levels of government in the rural development
process, with state and local governments assuming a more
active stance as the federal role diminishes. Thus, the
increasing recognition of the need for rural revitalization
and particularly of the changing nature of the economic forces
affecting rural areas has been the basis for a growing
research and public policy emphasis in recent years.

    The level of resources devoted to these issues has been
increasing, but progress is hampered by the difficulty
inherent in identifying and accessing relevant works in the
area. This difficulty stems in large measure from the
multidisciplinary nature of the subject, which results in
articles appearing in a wide variety of journals and report
series. An additional problem for those seeking an understanding of the process of economic decline and revitalization
is that, although much of the literature is found in readily
available professional journals or commercially published
texts, many of the most relevant works in the field consist of
special reports prepared by economic development organizations
or by agricultural experiment station or extension service
personnel, proceedings of conferences, or papers presented at
such conferences. Such documents can be very difficult to
identify. Thus, scholars and policymakers alike could benefit
from reference works that would help them readily identify key
works related directly to specific issues.

    The authors have previously completed three bibliog-
raphies related to, but not encompassing, this topic (see
items 67, 105, and 106 in this book). Readers may find these
bibliographies on plant closure, on the interdependencies of
agriculture and rural communities, and on assessing and
managing socioeconomic impacts equally useful as they try to
identify the nature and scope of rural economic decline and
assess the effects of policies, programs, and projects. Some
works from these previous efforts are included here, but the
vast majority of annotations in this book are new.

    The purpose of this book, then, is to bring together the
salient works on (1) the socioeconomic changes in rural
communities as a result of economic decline and (2) revitali-

zation strategies. The literature represented reviews the
economic, demographic, public service, fiscal, and social and
psychological effects of a declining economic base; examines a
variety of economic development strategies; and analyzes major
policy issues associated with economic decline and revitalization. The book is an attempt to meet the needs of (1)
students of community development, regional and agricultural
economics, community and regional planning, rural sociology,
and related disciplines; (2) teachers and researchers in the
academic community; and (3) policymakers and rural development
practitioners in both public and private sectors. The
specific elements of its focus and scope are discussed below.

Scope

As stated earlier, the focus of this book is on socioeconomic consequences of economic decline in rural areas and
strategies for the economic revitalization of the affected
communities. The scope of the book has been further narrowed
by examining problems of decline and revitalization only
within the world's industrialized countries. Therefore, the
compilers have concentrated on North American, European, and
Australian literature written in English.

Even though the current economic problems affecting rural
resource-dependent regions of the United States and of many
other countries have focused attention on economic decline and
revitalization, the problems are not new. Literature on the
topic appeared in the 1950s and 1960s, and some dates back to
the early 1900s. For purposes of this bibliography the
compilers concentrated their literature review on the period
1975-1987, although salient works written prior to 1975 were
reviewed if they were of enduring interest or formed the basis
of later research.

As the book was taking shape, several major topics became
apparent:

1. The socioeconomic and psychological consequences of
   economic decline (with considerable emphasis on adjustments of workers displaced by plant closings);
2. The effectiveness of various government policies aimed at
   preventing plant closings or providing more advance notice
   of such actions to affected workers and communities;
3. Strategies for economic development, including enhancing
   the efficiency of existing firms, improving an area's
   physical infrastructure and human capital, and analyzing

the effects of new industry and the factors influencing
the location of industry;

4. Sources of financing for rural development efforts;
5. Regional and local planning and the need for analytical
   models and data bases to assist planning efforts; and
6. Basic policy issues related to rural development efforts.

Methodology

A thorough search of socioeconomic and governmental
indexes and of pertinent professional journals yielded a rich
body of literature that was considered for inclusion in this
book. In addition, a computer bibliographic search was
conducted, and suggestions were solicited from leading
researchers. Criteria for inclusion of works included
methodological or empirical contribution, timeliness, and
availability.

Because research in this area has taken on a renewed
impetus, much of the literature on the topic has not yet made
its way into books and journal articles, but exists as
governmental reports and research reports issued by private
and public institutions. The compilers were careful to ensure
that works selected for this bibliography would be available
through libraries or universities or by writing directly to
specific agencies. A small body of material also exists as
unpublished papers presented at conferences and as disserta-
tions and theses. These works were included only if they were
available to the general public and contained useful material
not available elsewhere. Addresses of senior authors are
given to aid the researcher in acquiring these materials.

Organization of the Bibliography

The bibliography proper is organized into two broad
categories: (1) rural economic decline and (2) revitalization. The first category is subdivided into five sections:
demographic, economic, public service, and social and psychological effects, and policies and issues. The second section
is subdivided into six sections: general topics, improving
the efficiency of existing resources, expanding and diversifying the economic base, financing, planning and assessment, and
policies and issues.

Much care was taken to provide the reader with a well-
indexed book. The author index includes all authors and/or

editors, and the subject index includes key words from the
annotations. The subject index was difficult to construct
because of the seemingly endless opportunity to cross reference topics. Many cross references are provided, however, to
help the reader wade through the abundance of similar topics.
Because each annotation concerns either decline or revitalization, these two words rarely appear in the index. Theoreti-
cally, the entire subject index could be subsumed under these
two words. The reader is therefore instructed to think more
specifically when using the index. The reader should also
note that *the indexes use citation numbers and not page
numbers* when referring to location in the book.

Findings

The findings from the literature review reflect the recent
history and current status of research concerning economic
decline and revitalization of rural areas. Several major
themes are evident in the recent literature. One theme
concerns the various socioeconomic impacts of decline and the
need both for improved models and data bases to more accurately predict these impacts. Another theme is the efficacy of
specific policies advanced to assist communities and individuals affected by declining economic conditions. A third
theme addresses changes in the focus of rural development
efforts, with emphasis on the increasing importance of state
and local initiatives; on programs of local business retention, expansion, and creation; and on the role of nonmanufacturing businesses. Fourth is the need for expanded research
efforts to support the new rural development efforts.

Perhaps the most important finding is that one should not
overgeneralize concerning rural communities. National and
even regional averages can conceal great disparities in
economic structure, population characteristics, resource
endowments, and economic development potential. Nevertheless,
certain generalizations can be drawn from recent literature.
These findings are summarized in the paragraphs that follow.

The myriad impacts of economic decline are widely recog-
nized, but many of these impacts have not been the subject of
many detailed, empirical analyses. As a result, such important relationships as the magnitude of the secondary economic
multipliers associated with decline, the effect of reduced
employment opportunities on rates of labor force participation
and migration, and the effect of economic decline on property
values and local tax bases are not well understood. The few
efforts at empirical analysis reported to date, however,

indicate that the impacts of decline generally are not the mirror-opposite image of the impacts of growth. This, in turn, suggests that most empirical models developed to support local and regional planning (i.e., growth) may be of only limited utility in assessing the impacts of decline.

The appropriateness of various policy responses to problems of plant closure and economic decline has been the subject of intense debate. Some observers contend that legislation requiring firms to provide severance pay for workers and/or prenotification of closure intentions would substantially ease the adverse impacts associated with plant closings. Others argue, however, that such requirements would be detrimental to the firms involved, would discourage companies from establishing new operations in the jurisdiction in question, and would interfere with needed industrial restructuring and the free flow of capital.

Although many of the problems affecting rural communities with stagnant economies are long standing and in some cases have their origins in trends that have been evident for decades, some recent changes in the emphases of many rural development programs have become apparent. In particular, state and local governments appear to be taking an increasingly active role in economic revitalization efforts, and the role of the federal government has diminished. Economic development organizations appear to be placing a much greater emphasis on the retention and expansion of existing firms, on the creation of new local enterprises, and on the potential role of services and other nonmanufacturing activities in efforts to broaden an area's economic base.

Despite the widespread recognition that economic decline and stagnation is a major problem in many rural areas and that substantial development efforts will be required to reverse these patterns, major questions remain concerning the complex interrelations that are central to the process of economic development. For example, many states have made major commitments to programs of business retention and expansion, but analyses that measure the effectiveness of such programs do not appear to exist. Similarly, factors affecting industrial location and the role of small firms in job creation are still subjects of considerable debate. Likewise, while some observers indicate that services can play a substantial role in economic development programs, others suggest that the potential of the services sector in rural revitalization has been overrated. In general, more empirical analysis is needed to allow economic development practitioners to better understand the effectiveness of different development strategies under various conditions and thus to choose the most efficacious strategy for a given circumstance.

In closing, works annotated in this bibliography attest to the changing economic and population bases of rural areas and illustrate that there are substantial disparities in the characteristics and development potentials of rural areas. Formulating appropriate policy responses to changing economic conditions in such areas will require an in-depth understanding of the relationships that are central to patterns of economic growth and decline. It is critical that policymakers be aware of the far-reaching consequences of their actions, which in some cases may have the effect of exacerbating economic problems in rural areas. Evidence of renewed interest in these issues by both academicians and policymakers, however, offers hope that future rural development policies will be formulated in an enlightened atmosphere.

Community
Economic Decline

Demographic Effects

1. Beale, Calvin L. "Quantitative Dimensions of Decline and Stability Among Rural Communities." *Communities Left Behind: Alternatives for Development* (item 224), pp. 3-21.

   Summarizes the trends and discusses the implications of population growth and decline for rural towns and counties in the North Central region over the period 1940 to 1970.

2. Beale, Calvin L., and Glenn V. Fuguitt. *Metropolitan and Nonmetropolitan Growth Differentials in the United States Since 1980.* CDE Working paper 85-6. Madison, Wisc.: University of Wisconsin, Center for Demography and Ecology, 1985. 28 pp.

   Reports that in the first three years of the 1980s nonmetropolitan growth diminished to an annualized rate only about three-fifths as high as that of the 1970s, whereas metropolitan growth has continued its previous pace. Although the force of the agricultural and industrial recession of 1980-1983 in nonmetropolitan areas produced much of this change, nonmetropolitan counties with previous growth linked to retirement (and thus protected from income decline) have similarly slowed their rate of growth. The authors conclude that the strength of the noneconomic, quality-of-life objectives that attracted people to rural and small town communities in the 1970s may have waned and that economic recovery in these areas may not lead to a full resumption of the pattern of population growth found in the 1970s.

3. Clawson, Marion. "Restoration of the Quality of Life in Rural America." *Externalities in the Transformation of Agriculture: Distribution of Benefits and Costs from Development.* Ames, Iowa: Iowa State University Press, 1975. pp. 178-95.

Examines consequences of continued population loss in
rural areas. Effects noted include outmigration,
specially among the younger, better-educated
individuals; loss of customers for local businesses;
higher per capita costs for services; loss of service
quality; and declining asset values in rural towns.

4. Cook, Annabel Kirschner. *Population Change in Local
   Areas*. WREP 93. Corvallis, Ore.: Oregon State
   University, Western Rural Development Center, 1986.
   15 pp.
   Discusses population processes that produce growth or
   decline in an area and some implications of those
   processes. National trends, which may affect the
   population characteristics of local areas, are discussed, and key sources of demographic data are
   described.

5. DaVanzo, Julie. "Does Unemployment Affect Migration?--
   Evidence from MicroData." *The Review of Economics and
   Statistics* 60, no. 4 (1978): 504-14.
   Tests five hypotheses about how employment status
   affects the importance of various migration determinants. Results indicate that families whose heads are
   unemployed or dissatisfied with their jobs are more
   likely to move than those not searching for different
   jobs, that recent arrivals who cannot find acceptable
   jobs are especially prone to move, that job market
   information might discourage unproductive moves, that
   policies of investment to expand economic opportunities
   in depressed areas are likely to prevent economically
   forced outmigration, and that unemployed persons are
   more responsive to other economic determinants of
   migration (i.e., family income, origin, wage rates, and
   expected earnings increases) than persons satisfied with
   their jobs.

6. Fuguitt, Glenn V. "County Seat Status as a Factor in
   Small Town Growth and Decline." *Social Forces* 44
   (1965): 245-51.
   Uses data for all nonmetropolitan places in the United
   States outside New England for the period 1940-1960 to
   test the hypothesis that county seats are more likely to
   grow than other small towns. With size of place con-
   trolled, the hypothesis was true for towns in the South
   and in the North away from metropolitan centers, but not
   in the West.

7. Fuguitt, Glenn V. "The Places Left Behind: Population Trends and Policy for Rural America." *Rural Sociology* 36, no. 3 (1971): 449-70.
    Analyzes population changes in rural incorporated places between 1950 and 1970. Results indicate an emerging decentralization trend around larger nonmetropolitan centers, and regions of the country showed marked differences in some patterns of population change.

8. Hamilton, Joel R. "Population Change and Retail Sales Patterns in Local Authority Areas of Queensland." *Review of Marketing and Agricultural Economics* 50, no. 1 (1982): 97-108.
    Uses census data from Queensland to test whether or not the relationships between population and retail trade patterns derived from central place theory were applicable at the local authority level. Larger local authorities achieve higher per capita retail sales than less populous places, and proximity to larger centers reduces per capita sales. Population growth allows a local authority to capture a higher proportion of spending locally, while decline encourages and even forces people to shop elsewhere.

9. Hart, John Fraser, Neil E. Salisbury, and Everett G. Smith, Jr. "The Dying Village and Some Notions About Urban Growth." *Economic Geography* 44, no. 4 (October 1968): 343-49.
    Points out that most villages of 250 to 1,000 persons in the Midwest are not dying, but are continuing to grow in population, despite their obvious loss of many of their former economic functions. Using extensive field interviews in more than thirty villages scattered over four states and using less highly structured field work in many other villages, the authors examine some of the implications of the fact of village growth for theories about urban growth.

10. Herzog, Henry W., Jr., and Alan M. Schlottmann. "Labor Force Mobility in the United States: Migration, Unemployment, and Remigration." *International Regional Science Review* 9, no. 1 (1984): 43-58.
    Examines the relationships between pre- and postmove unemployment and interstate migration of the United States labor force for the period 1965-1970. Multivariate analyses were conducted for several large occupation groups. The results indicate a strong link

between unemployment and migration. Unemployment
increases migration possibilities for each large
occupation group considered. Substantial postmove
unemployment exists, but there is a significant link
between migration and such unemployment only for blue-
collar workers who are repeat migrants.

11. Johansen, Harley E., and Glenn V. Fuguitt. "Changing
     Retail Activity in Wisconsin Villages: 1939-1954-
     1970." *Rural Sociology* 38, no. 2 (1973): 207-18.
     Presents an analysis of change in retail and service
activities in a sample of Wisconsin villages, documents
trends in trade activities by village, and reviews the
patterns of change by individual functions.

12. Johansen, Harley E., and Glenn V. Fuguitt. "Population
     Growth and Retail Decline: Conflicting Effects of
     Urban Accessibility in American Villages." *Rural
     Sociology* 44, no. 1 (1979): 24-38.
     Uses a path model and multiple regression to examine
the relationship between urban accessibility and business change in rural villages. The weak association
between urban accessibility and retail change is due to
a negative direct effect of accessibility on retail
change being offset by a positive indirect effect
operating through population change.

13. Johnson, Kenneth M. *The Impact of Population Change on
     Business Activity in Rural America*. Boulder,
     Colorado: Westview Press, 1985. 180 pp.
     Moves beyond existing literature on rural-urban
population shifts during the past forty years to examine
the effects of those shifts on the business infrastructure that supplies goods and services to rural areas in
the United States. First establishing the historical
demographic context, the author provides a detailed
longitudinal treatment on the linkage between population
change and the rural commercial infrastructure, as well
as timely information on the impact of the recent rural
population turnaround on business. Some of the findings
refute earlier expectations that a decrease in
population necessarily leads to a decline in the local
business community.

14. Kale, Steven. "Factors Associated with Population
     Change in Rural Areas." *Journal of Community
     Development Society* 7, no. 2 (1976): 41-58.

Employs a regression model to investigate the role of selected variables associated with 1960 to 1970 population change for 211 Nebraska communities with populations between 400 and 9,999 in 1960. Independent variables examined were urban proximity, size of center in 1960, government activity, traffic flow, manufacturing activity, farm density, community development, irrigation activity, and housing supply.

15. Kale, Steven. "Small Town Population Change in the Central Great Plains: An Investigation of Recent Trends." *Rocky Mountain Social Sciences Journal* 12, (1975): 29-43.
Examines the areal pattern and spatial extent of recent small town growth and decline in the central Great Plains. Trends of population decline in smaller trade centers are noted.

16. Montague, Meg. "Internal Migration and Rural Depopulation." *Planning in Turbulent Environments*. Edited by John S. Western and Paul R. Wilson. St. Lucia, Queensland, Australia: University of Queensland Press, 1977. pp. 163-82.
Investigates the sociological features of population movement from a rural shire in central western Queensland. A brief overview of the area and its population is presented before the description of the exresidents and the discussion of differential factors operating in the process by which they became migrants, their motivation for migrating, and their eventual destination.

17. Murdock, Steve H., Rita R. Hamm, Lloyd Potter, and Don Albrecht. "Demographic Characteristics of Rural Residents in Financial Distress and Social and Community Impacts of the Farm Crisis." *The Farm Financial Crisis: Socioeconomic Dimensions and Implications for Producers and Rural Areas* (item 118).
Examines the demographic characteristics of producers with different levels of debt, farmers who quit due to the crisis, and former business persons in rural communities. The authors then examine their opinions on the crisis, on its impacts on their personal lives, and on the businesses and services in their communities.

18. National Fertilizer Development Center. *The Labor Force: Migration, Earnings, and Growth*. Bull. Y-63. Muscle Shoals, Ala., 1973. 132 pp. (Doc. Y3.T25: 3-2/Y-63)

Presents the proceedings of a symposium to bring
together researchers and others interested in using the
Social Security Administration's Continuous Work History
Sample, one of the first longitudinal data sources on
migration and economic growth. Topics of papers presented at the symposium include rural outmigration,
migration and its effect on agriculture and rural development, future growth of the Southeast, and
interindustry mobility.

19. Scott, Peter. "Agricultural Change and Rural Stability
     in Australia." *The Effect of Modern Agriculture on
     Rural Development*. New York: Pergamon Press, 1982.
     pp. 65-84.
     Focuses on recent changes in farm numbers and in rural
     population against a background of the changing
     enterprise structure of Australian farming in response
     to changing cost-price relationships. Scott pays
     particular attention to the intercensal period 1966-
     1971 when the rural sector underwent the greatest
     upheaval of any postwar intercensal period.

20. Taves, Marvin J. "Consequences of Population Loss in
     Rural Communities." *Labor Mobility and Population in
     Agriculture*. Ames, Iowa: Iowa State University Press,
     1961. pp. 107-21.
     Examines the effects of outmigration on rural communi-
     ties first in a historical context and then by type of
     community resident (youth, production outmigrant aged
     twenty-five to sixty, and older outmigrant).

21. U.S. Department of Labor. *Displaced Workers, 1979-83*.
     Bull. 2240. Washington, D.C.: Government Printing
     Office, July 1985. 29 pp.
     Describes displaced workers by age, sex, race, indus-
     try, occupation, geographic location, reason for job
     loss, length of unemployment, prenotification, and re-
     employment characteristics. The study focuses on
     workers who had been employed at least three years
     before being terminated or laid off.

Economic Effects

22. Adams, Bert N. "The Small Trade Center: Processes and
     Perceptions of Growth or Decline." *The Community: A
     Comparative Perspective*. Edited by Robert Mills

French. Itasca, Ill.: F.E. Peacock Publishers, 1969.
pp. 471-84.
Examines the internal conditions contributing to
individual or community stability, to the stages in the
loss of services in a declining village, and to people's
perceptions of small town economic conditions. Six farm
trade centers (two in Missouri and four in Wisconsin)
were selected for investigation.

23. Advisory Commission on Intergovernmental Relations.
     Regional Growth: Historic Perspective. Washington,
     D.C., June 1980. 143 pp. (Doc. Y3.Ad9/8: 2R26/4/v.1)
     Examines the economic growth of the various regions of
the United States and points out the importance of the
converging growth rates throughout the nation. The
report specifically addresses the geographical disper-
sion of economic activity, determinants of regional
shifts, and government policy and financial assistance.

24. Agricultural Policy Institute. *Creating Opportunities
     for Tomorrow.* Raleigh, N.C.: North Carolina State
     University, School of Agriculture and Life Sciences,
     1968. 152 pp.
     Discusses the implications and recommendations of the
report of the President's National Advisory Commission
on Rural Poverty. Various authors discuss where people
will live and work in the future, investments needed to
prepare people for effective roles in society, improving
communities, government services, and employment opportunities in declining rural areas.

25. *The Annals of the American Academy of Political and
     Social Science.* Special Issue: *Deindustrialization:
     Restructuring the Economy.* Edited by Gene F. Summers.
     Vol. 475 (September 1984). 174 pp.
     Focuses on three aspects of the deindustrialization
debate: the nature of restructuring, its effects on
workers and communities, and alternative policy options
to deal with economic restructuring. Articles describ-
ing recent experiences in Sweden and Britain provide a
comparative perspective.

26. Aronson, Robert L., and Robert B. McKersie. *Economic
     Consequences of Plant Shutdowns in New York State.*
     Ithaca, N.Y.: Cornell University, 1980. 171 pp.
     Provides an overview of the problems involved in a
shutdown and points out the need for further development
of human resources policy. Three communities in New

York were studied as the basis for this report. The
primary focus is on the community-level or macro-effects
and adjustments to the economic trauma. The authors
also review worker adjustment and behavior.

27. Arrowhead Regional Development Commission. *Economic*
     Adjustment Strategies: In the Event of the Loss of a
     Major Regional Employer. Duluth, Minn.: Arrowhead
     Regional Development Commission, 1977. 289 pp.
     Prepared in response to the potential court-ordered
closure of the Reserve Mining Company of Silver Bay,
Minnesota. The firm employed 2,870 persons in 1977.
The threatened closure would bring about economic and
social disaster for seven communities and nine town-
ships, as well as have lesser effects on all of northeastern Minnesota. Topics covered in the report include
methodology; regional setting; state and federal responses; job placement, retraining, and income maintenance; housing investment protection; local governmental
services maintenance; business and commercial strategies; and growth impacts and related economic
adjustments.

28. Arthur, Louise M., and David Freshwater. *Analysis of*
     the Economic Effects of a Prolonged Agricultural
     Drought In Manitoba: Summary Report. Res. Bull. No.
     86-2. Winnipeg, Manitoba: University of Manitoba,
     Dept. Agr. Econ. and Farm Mgmt., 1986. 174 pp.
     Assesses the current sensitivity of the Manitoba
economy to major droughts, which impact agricultural
production. Various scenarios that involved changes in
cultivation practices (including irrigation) were examined under normal and drought weather conditions to
determine the effectiveness of these alternatives in
stabilizing the Manitoba economy during periods of
prolonged drought. The economic development effects of
the alternative scenarios also were examined.

29. Ayer, Harry W., and M. Ross Layton. "Meeting the
     Economic Impact of Mine-Smelter Phase-Down in Bisbee-
     Douglas." *Arizona Review* 21, no. 12 (December 1972):
     1-5.
     Uses 1960 and 1965 data and an input-output model of
Cochise County to estimate the impact on employment,
population, and value added of the mine-smelter phase-
down and redevelopment proposals.

30. Bale, Malcolm D., and Diane P. Miller. *The Effects of
     Adjustment Assistance on Trade-Displaced Workers: A
     Case Study.* Bozeman, Mont.: Montana State University,
     1976. 75 pp.
     Attempts to determine the effects of the timing of
     receipt of trade assistance upon worker adjustment.
     Chosen as the experimental group were workers who
     received adjustment assistance within one month of
     layoff. The control group were workers who received
     assistance more than one year after the layoff. The
     authors used two multiple regression models to compare
     worker adjustment.

31. Barkley, Paul W., and Joanne Buteau. *The Economics of
     Rural Businessmen: A Case Study in Lincoln County,
     Washington.* WRDC Discussion Paper No. 3. Corvallis,
     Ore.: Oregon State University, Western Rural
     Development Center, 1974. 22 pp.
     Reports preliminary findings from a study of forty-
     three businessmen located in several small agricultural
     trade centers in east central Washington. Results
     suggest that, while some business opportunity remains in
     these towns, the capital values of most businesses'
     assets are declining, their clientele groups are
     becoming smaller, and they feel increased pressure from
     government regulations, cooperative stores, and tax-
     exempt properties in their towns. Their adaptive
     strategies vary by size of place, type of business, and
     age of operator.

32. Beck, Roger, and William Herr. *Effects of Farm Sector
     Recession on Retail Sales and Nonfarm Income in Rural
     Illinois Counties.* Carbondale, Ill.: Southern
     Illinois University, Dept. of Agribusiness Econ.,
     1986. 11 pp.
     Uses retail sales and wage and salary data to examine
     linkages between farm and various nonfarm sectors in
     Illinois counties. The authors demonstrate the direct
     impact of the farm recession on retail sales and the
     secondary impacts on income originating in selected
     dependent sectors (e.g., retail, services, finance).

33. Belongia, Michael T., and R. Alton Gilbert. "The Farm
     Credit Crisis: Will It Hurt the Whole Economy?"
     Review (The Federal Reserve Bank of St. Louis) 67, no.
     10 (1985): 5-15.
     Makes some comparisons and contrasts between the farm

financial crisis of the 1920s and the 1980s and
discusses the implications for the economy as a whole.

34. Berglind, Hans. "Unemployment and Redundancy in a 'Post
    Industrial' Labor Market." *Work and Technology*.
    Edited by Marie R. Haug and Jacques Dofny. Beverly
    Hills, Calif.: Sage Publications, 1977. pp. 195-213.
    Discusses Sweden's transition to a postindustrial
    economy in which the service sector plays a more
    dominant role in labor force employment. Berglind
    presents data indicating that the number of redundant
    people has grown markedly during the last decade. Some
    alternative reasons for the fact are discussed along
    with the risks of a more segregated society in which a
    growing number of economically inefficient people will
    be unemployed and dependent upon the rest of the
    population for economic support.

35. Bergman, Edward R., and Kenny Johnson. *Rural
    Flight/Urban Might: Economic Development Challenges
    for the 1980s*. Report of the 1986 Commission on the
    Future of the South. Research Triangle Park, N.C.:
    The Southern Growth Priorities Board, 1987. 28 pp.
    Reviews and analyzes recent patterns of economic
    growth and decline in the southeastern United States.

36. Bluestone, Barry, and Bennett Harrison. *The
    Deindustrialization of America: Plant Closings,
    Community Abandonment, and the Dismantling of Basic
    Industry*. New York: Basic Books, 1982. 323 pp.
    Documents the widespread closure of manufacturing
    plants in the United States, analyzes the reasons for
    and consequences of plant closings, and proposes a new
    industrial strategy, which the authors call "reindus-
    trialization with a human face," with such objectives as
    the equitable sharing of economic growth, production of
    useful goods and services, a humane work environment,
    and economic democracy. In the short term, they support
    rebuilding the social safety net and the passage of
    plant-closing legislation.

37. Bluestone, Herman, and Mindy Petrulis. "Falling Energy
    Prices Hurt Rural Mining Counties." *Rural Development
    Perspectives* 3, no. 3 (June 1987): 39-40.
    Examines the real per capita income and unemployment
    rates in mining-dependent counties in the United States.

38. Boody, George, and Michael Rivard. *Economic and Social Vulnerability in Rural Minnesota: An Urgent Needs and Resource Assessment.* Final Report to the Rural Strategy Task Force. Minneapolis, Minn.: The Rural Enterprise Institute, 1986. 35 pp. plus appendixes.
Tracks the impacts of the farm crisis in rural Minnesota and identifies additional negative economic forces that may worsen the crisis. The concept of vulnerability is used to tie together dynamics of economic shock, social suffering, cumulative emotional distress, and population displacement. Central to the discussion are the structural changes taking place in farming and the rural economy.

39. Bowen, Richard L., and David L. Foster. *A Profile of Displaced Pineapple Workers on Moloka'i.* Research Extension Series 031. Honolulu: University of Hawaii, College of Tropical Agriculture and Human Resources, 1983. 24 pp.
Summarizes a survey of workers being terminated as Del Monte Corporation shut down its pineapple operations on the island of Moloka'i. Information obtained included demographics, assets, sources of income, plans for relocation or retirement, present occupation, skill areas, future employment interests, and perceived needs for support services.

40. Bradbury, John H., and Isabelle St. Martin. "Winding Down in a Quebec Mining Town: A Case Study of Schefferville." *Canadian Geographer* 27, no. 2 (1983): 128-44.
Examines the pattern of decline in a mining region using a case study of Schefferville. A critical examination is made of Lucas's model of youth to maturity in community development, and two more stages are suggested--winding down and closing a town. The discussion centers on the characteristics of community and corporate winding down in Schefferville: the restructuring of the local workforce; disinvestment; relocation of capital; and company withdrawal from housing, municipal affairs, and public services.

41. Brake, John R., ed. *Emerging and Projected Trends Likely to Influence the Structure of Midwest Agriculture, 1970-1985.* Monograph No. 11. Iowa City, Iowa: University of Iowa, College of Law, Agricultural Law Center, 1970. 126 pp.

Collects seven articles on the future of agriculture:
(1) size, efficiency, and organization of the production
unit in Midwestern agriculture in the 1980s; (2) capitalizing agriculture; (3) intergenerational transfer of
farm wealth; (4) the impact of trends in farm production
units on input-supply industries; (5) trends in the food
industries; (6) the impacts of trends on community and
human welfare; and (7) the aggregate impact of trends on
the economy and the agriculture industry as a whole.
Contains items 56, 221, and 231.

42. Braschler, Curtis H., and Martha Sieberling. "Impacts
     of the Farm Crisis on the Missouri Economy and Some
     Selected Rural Counties 1977-1984." *Economic &*
     Marketing Information 29, no. 9 (September 1986): 1-4.
     Examines the growth of income and employment based on
actual growth in agricultural sales as compared to the
expected state growth in agriculture, if the trend of
the late 1970s had continued.

43. Brownrigg, Mark. "Industrial Contraction and the
     Regional Multiplier Effect: An Application in
     Scotland." *Town Planning Review* 51, no. 2 (1980):
     195-210.
     Analyzes a typical situation of threatened economic
contraction in western Scotland, in the form of the
impending closure or severe rationalization of a manufacturing plant in Kilmarnock. The author's objectives
are (1) to provide quantitative estimates of the possible repercussions of the plant contraction on employment in other linked industries and in the local
services sector as a result of falling income and
expenditure levels locally, and (2) to evaluate the
unique circumstances associated with industrial decline
and determine the extent to which these must be incorporated by modifications into the employment multiplier
model.

44. Burke, Ronald J. "Comparison of Experiences of Men and
     Women Following a Plant Shutdown." *Psychological*
     Reports 57 (1985): 59-66.
     Compares the experiences of 155 men and 22 women who
lost their jobs when the Canadian Admiral plant in
Ontario closed. Data were collected sixteen months
after closure. Generally, women were relatively
disadvantaged; fewer found new jobs and those who did
were earning significantly lower wages than men.

45. Burton, Dudley J., and Irvine Alpert. "The Decline of
    California's North Coast Redwood Region." *Policy
    Studies Journal* 10, no. 2 (1981): 272-84.
    Examines the theoretical, political, and environmental
    problems with the range of regional responses to eco-
    nomic decline in the redwood region of northern
    California.

46. California Department of Economic and Business
    Development. *Buyout: A Guide for Workers Facing Plant
    Closings*. Sacramento, 1983. 80 pp.
    Describes steps to determine the feasibility of
    avoiding plant closures and preserving long-term jobs.
    The first part discusses employee ownership, includes
    examples of such an option, and describes the union's
    role in an employee-owned company. The second part is a
    guide to investigating employee ownership, factors for
    success, and steps in preparing a feasibility study.
    Numerous checklists are included. Appendixes include
    technical assistance references, a list of films on
    plant closures and worker ownership, and suggestions on
    organizing a buyout committee.

47. California Employment Development Department. *Planning
    Guidebook for Communities Facing a Plant Closure or
    Mass Layoff*. Sacramento: State of California, 1983.
    176 pp.
    Designs a framework to provide communities with a
    response program to deal with closure of a major
    business. Section one introduces the problem of
    closures and outlines the recent history of California's
    efforts to understand and mitigate the worst effects of
    closures. Section two presents a detailed description
    of the organization of a community response program and
    provides guidelines for the development of a community
    committee and a re-employment center. Section three
    focuses on the state's experience in developing
    retraining programs and highlights successful components
    of programs developed throughout the state.

48. Casner-Lott, Jill. "Plant Closings, Relocations In-
    crease: Federal Regulation Proposed to Reduce
    Disruption to Communities, Employees." *World of Work
    Report* 4, no. 12 (December 1979): 89, 93.
    Discusses the reasons for plant closings and addresses
    the pros and cons of government intervention and legis-
    lation. Also, alternatives to legislation are
    discussed. Tax and financial incentives for companies,

reducing the work force gradually, and advance notice to
alert workers and the community are some of the ideas
under consideration.

49. Centre for Resource Studies. *Mining Communities: Hard
     Lessons For the Future.* Kingston, Ontario: Queen's
     University, 1984. 205 pp.
     Contains the proceedings of a policy discussion
seminar on the problems posed by mine closures and
shutdowns in Canada. Emphasis was placed on new
planning approaches that are being designed to avoid
single-industry dependence and to share financial risks.
Contains nine papers and a digest of discussions.

50. Chalmers, James A., and Michael J. Greenwood. "The
     Regional Labor Market Adjustment Process: Determinants
     of Changes in Rates of Labor Force Participation,
     Unemployment, and Migration." *Annals of Regional
     Science* 19, no. 1 (1985): 1-17.
     Employs a simultaneous-equations model to examine the
regional labor market adjustment process for a sample of
United States counties over the 1960-1970 period. The
interaction between employment change and migration is
well known, but the intervention between employment
change and labor force participation has been largely
neglected. Labor force participation response,
especially among women, is shown to be an important
endogenous element in the labor market adjustment
process. Important asymmetries are also evident between
growing and declining regions, and these asymmetries
suggest that the well-established link between
employment and migration may have more force in growing
than in declining areas.

51. Clawson, Marion. "The Dying Community: The Natural
     Resource Base." *The Dying Community*. Edited by Art
     Gallaher, Jr. and Harland Padfield. Albuquerque,
     N.M.: University of New Mexico Press, 1980. pp. 55-
     83.
     Discusses the relationship between natural resources
and the growth and decline of nearby communities.
Clawson states that, if a resource-based community has
lost its economic relevance, there may be little the
community can do about it. In other cases, communities
can sometimes find new resources, can find new ways to
use old resources, or can attract new industries not
dependent on geographic location.

52. Congressional Budget Office. *Dislocated Workers: Issues and Federal Options*. Washington, D.C.: Congress of the United States, 1982. 56 pp.
    Examines problems facing workers displaced by structural changes in the economy, who often face particular difficulty adjusting to changed employment demands and thus often experience longer-than-usual periods of unemployment. Whether the federal government should provide special assistance to such workers and what form any aid might take are issues examined in this study.

53. Corden, W. Max, and J. Peter Neary. "Booming Sector and De-Industrialisation in a Small Open Economy." *The Economic Journal* 92 (December 1982): 825-48.
    Attempts to provide a systematic analysis of some aspects of structural change in an open economy. In particular, it examines what is called "Dutch disease": the coexistence within the traded goods sector of progressing and declining, or booming and lagging, subsectors. The authors examine the sources and effects of a boom, then examine the effects when labor is the only mobile factor and when capital is mobile between two or three sectors.

54. Cottrell, William F. "Death by Dieselization: A Case Study in the Reaction to Technology Change." *American Sociological Review* 16, no. 3 (1951): 358-65.
    Examines changing attitudes and values of the residents in a one-industry railroad town faced with the termination of railroad activities. Attitudes changed from viewing the railroad company as an employer concerned with the community to one concerned only with the bottom line. Collective action became the key to survival. Unions and the community joined together to ensure retention of existing union rules and adoption of new rules and government regulations.

55. Cumberland, John H. "Dimensions of the Impact of Reduced Military Expenditures on Industries, Regions, and Communities." *The Economic Consequences of Reduced Military Spending* (item 151), pp. 79-147.
    Examines the nature of regional economic impacts, methods for measuring and projecting regional impacts, and alternative public policy approaches for dealing with problems of regional economic adjustment to reduced military spending.

56. Dahl, Dale C. "The Impact of Trends in Farm Production
    Units on the Input-Supplying Industries." *Emerging
    and Projected Trends Likely to Influence the Structure
    of Midwest Agriculture, 1970-1985* (item 41), pp. 74-
    85.
    Reviews some of the recent changes in organization and
    firm strategy in several farm-supply industry markets,
    both at the manufacturing or primary-producing level and
    at the retail level, and suggests future patterns of
    change in these industries. Dahl limits his discussion
    to such industries as fertilizer, chemicals, petroleum,
    feed, machinery, and credit.

57. Daicoff, Darwin W. "The Adjustment of DOD Civilian and
    Military Personnel." *The Economic Consequences of
    Reduced Military Spending* (item 151), pp. 167-77.
    Examines the transition of civilian and military
    personnel into the workforce after the cessation of the
    war in Vietnam. Military personnel are expected to
    experience more severe adjustment problems because their
    skills are often highly specialized and not readily
    transferable.

58. Daicoff, Darwin W. "The Community Impact of Military
    Installations." *The Economic Consequences of Reduced
    Military Spending* (item 151), pp. 149-66.
    Analyzes the impact of a new or expanded installation
    or the impact of a reduction or closure of an estab-
    lished base on adjacent communities. Specifically, the
    author considers impact studies of military installation
    location, relocation, or discontinuation that have
    occurred from 1960 to 1973.

59. Dean, Lois. "Minersville: A Study in Socioeconomic
    Stagnation." *Human Organization* 24 (1965): 254-61.
    Describes the insularity, alienation, and languor
    found among the leadership of Minersville, a community
    in a state of socioeconomic stagnation and indifferent
    to economic growth. These attitudes are an impediment
    to economic planning and are probably most solidly
    entrenched in the areas that stand to benefit most from
    the consequences of economic planning.

60. Devens, Richard M., Jr. "Displaced Workers: One Year
    Later." *Monthly Labor Review* 109 (July 1986): 40-44.
    Reports on changes in labor market status of displaced
    workers between January 1984 and January 1985. Nation-
    wide, 71 percent of the displaced men and 61 percent of

the women were employed in January 1985, compared to 64
percent of the men and 53 percent of the women a year
earlier.

61. DiNoto, Michael, and Larry Merk. *The Economic Status of
     Shoshone County, Idaho: A Post-Mortem or Period of
     Transition*. Moscow, Idaho: University of Idaho,
     Department of Economics, 1983.
     Examines the economic consequences of the closure of
the Bunker Hill Company mine near Kellogg, Idaho, in
which 2,100 workers lost their job in 1982.

62. Doeksen, Gerald A. "The Agricultural Crisis As It
     Affects Rural Communities." *Journal of the Community
     Development Society* 18, no. 1 (1987): 78-88.
     Uses a simulation model to illustrate how the farm
crisis is expected to affect rural businesses and
governments. The crisis is and will continue to occur
in many rural communities as long as farmers are
liquidating their farming operations. When farmers are
forced to quit, they look for off-farm jobs. If none
are available, they will be forced to move to urban
centers for employment. As they move, rural businesses
will have fewer sales and local governments will have
fewer dollars. In the case of rural businesses, some
will be forced to close and others will operate with
less income. With regard to local governments, fewer
tax dollars will be available, and services may have to
be reduced.

63. Doeksen, Gerald A., John Kuehn, and Joseph Schmidt.
     "Consequences of Decline and Community and Economic
     Adjustment To It." *Communities Left Behind:
     Alternatives for Development* (item 224), pp. 28-42.
     Attempts to (1) delineate the economic dynamics of
rural communities, (2) rationalize the reactions of
economic institutions given the historical settings, and
(3) consider the economic outlook for rural communities.

64. Doeksen, Gerald A., and Mike D. Woods. *The Inter-
     dependence of Basic Industries with Rural Communities:
     How Economists Can Help*. AE-8714. Stillwater, Okla.:
     Oklahoma State University, Department of Agricultural
     Economics, 1987. 24 pp.
     Illustrates how a community simulation model can be
used to measure how the impact of a change in basic
economic activity will affect the economic health of a
rural community. Results of two applications of the

simulation model are presented: (1) a situation where a
manufacturing plant closed and (2) a region having a
reduction of farmers by 20 percent.

65. Drabenstott, Mark, and Lynn Gibson. *Rural America In
    Transition*. Kansas City, Mo.: Federal Reserve Bank of
    Kansas City, 1987.
    Represents a compilation of research conducted at the
    Federal Reserve Bank of Kansas City. Five major chap-
    ters address the fundamental economic transition under-
    way in the rural economy and discuss the important
    policy questions related to the transition.

66. Dunkle, Robert, Deborah Brown, and Stephen Lovejoy.
    "Adaptation Strategies of Main-Street Merchants." *The
    Rural Sociologist* 3, no. 2 (1983): 102-6.
    Presents some preliminary findings of a two-year study
    of two rural communities in north central Indiana. The
    authors comment on the relationship between the strat-
    egies of merchants to survive and the level of community
    decline.

67. Ekstrom, Brenda L., and F. Larry Leistritz. *Plant
    Closure and Community Economic Decline*. Public
    Administration Series, Bibliography P 1887.
    Monticello, Ill.: Vance Bibliographies, 1986.   47 pp.
    Annotates 138 items on the social, economic, and
    psychological consequences of plant closure and
    community decline in the United States, Canada, Great
    Britain, and Western Europe.

68. Erickson, Jon. *Plant Closings: Impact, Causes, and
    Policies*. No. 127. Chicago: CPL Bibliographies,
    November 1983.
    Is a five-part annotated bibliography containing
    general works on the topic; studies on the impact of
    closure on workers and communities, on the causes of
    closure in the United States and Europe, and on policy
    initiatives; and historical accounts dating back to the
    Depression. The work contains 168 entries.

69. Erickson, Rodney A. "Corporate Organization and Manu-
    facturing Branch Plant Closures in Non-Metropolitan
    Areas." *Regional Studies* 14 (1980): 491-501.
    Examines the hypothesis that branch plants in
    nonmetropolitan areas, because they are relatively easy
    to establish, are more likely to close during a reces-
    sion or financial difficulties. Data on the performance

of a large set of plants in nonmetropolitan Wisconsin indicate that such branches are far less likely to close than establishments in general. The article also examines the influences of alternative corporate organizational structures and related plant interdependencies, market environments, levels of capital investment, and acquisition on branch closure rates.

70. Fairchild, Charles K. *Worker Relocation: A Review of U.S. Department of Labor Mobility Demonstration Projects.* Washington, D.C.: E.F. Shelley and Co., 1970. 175 pp.
    Reviews the experience of labor mobility demonstration projects and makes recommendations concerning issues and techniques in the design and operation of a broader, permanent worker-relocation program. The demonstration projects are viewed as providing valuable experience that could be utilized to develop guidelines for the design and operation of a nationwide program.

71. Fedrau, Ruth. "A Comprehensive State Response to Plant Closings and Mass Layoffs." *The Entrepreneurial Economy* (November 1982): 7-9.
    Relates the efforts of California to assist displaced workers. The California Economic Adjustment Team created fourteen reemployment centers that offered comprehensive adjustment assistance to nearly 30,000 displaced workers in the state.

72. Flaim, Paul O., and Ellen Sehgal. "Displaced Workers of 1979-83: How Well have They Fared?" *Monthly Labor Review* (June 1985): 3-16.
    Reports the findings of a special household survey conducted in 1984 by the U.S. Department of Labor to identify workers who had lost their jobs during the 1980-81 and 1982-83 recessions due to plant closings, employers going out of business, and layoffs from which the worker was not recalled.

73. Ginder, Roger G., Kenneth E. Stone, and Daniel Otto. "Impact of the Farm Financial Crisis on Agribusiness Firms and Rural Communities." *American Journal of Agricultural Economics* 67, no. 5 (1985): 1184-90.
    Investigates the implications of the farm financial crisis for rural communities--agribusiness, main street businesses, and the various community institutions, such

as schools and churches. The article focuses on impacts
in Iowa and the upper Midwest.

74. Glover, Glenn H. "Agribusiness in the Agricultural
     Financial Crisis." *Southern Journal of Agricultural
     Economics* 18, no. 1 (1986): 103-12.
     Examines the current financial situation in agricul-
     ture, identifies factors that have contributed to it,
     and explores alternative strategies for agribusiness
     firms.

75. Gordus, Jeanne P., Paul Jarley, and Louis A. Ferman.
     Plant Closing and Economic Dislocation. Kalamazoo,
     Mich.: W.E. Upjohn Institute for Employment Research,
     1981. 173 pp.
     Provides a comprehensive review of the plant-closing
     research undertaken over the past two decades. The
     authors attempt to identify conceptual and methodo-
     logical limitations of past research, areas where policy
     needs to be developed, and directions in which
     programming efforts should move. The book is intended
     as a compendium of information which could promote the
     formulation of a new research agenda and assist
     policymakers and planners who might wish to review past
     efforts in order to find directions for the present and
     future.

76. Gordus, Jeanne Prial. "The Human Resource Implications
     of Plant Shutdowns." *The Annals of the American
     Academy of Political and Social Science* 475 (September
     1984): 66-79.
     Examines the fragmented efforts to develop human
     resource programs to aid in job placement, job search,
     relocation, and retraining of displaced workers. Much
     of the recent effort seems to be focused on training and
     placement of the most advantaged displaced workers, so
     that less-advantaged displaced workers are often
     consigned to underemployment, permanent unemployment, or
     eventual dependence upon income maintenance.

77. Gulliford, Andrew. "From Boom to Bust: Small Towns and
     Energy Development on Colorado's Western Slope."
     Small Town 13, no. 5 (1983): 15-22.
     Describes the rapid economic growth, and equally rapid
     decline, associated with oil shale development in
     western Colorado. Discussion centers on the abandonment
     of the Colony Oil Shale project and the effects of this
     shutdown on small towns in Garfield County.

78. Gutteridge, Thomas G. "Labor Market Adaptations of
     Displaced Technical Professionals." *Industrial and
     Labor Relations Review* 31, no. 4 (July 1978): 460-73.
     Tests a decision model for displaced workers--that
     length of time unemployed is a function of salary,
     occupational, and geographical area aspirations--on a
     random sample of about 3,000 unemployed engineers and
     scientists. Results indicate that after a sustained
     period of unemployment, these professionals were more
     willing than initially to change occupations but not
     geographic areas, and those who originally were un-
     willing to accept a salary reduction actually increased
     their salary expectations, but those originally willing
     to take a pay cut decreased their salary aspirations by
     ten percent. Professed aspirations were more strongly
     related than demographic and work history variables to
     actual behavior.

79. Hansen, Gary B. "Preventing Layoffs: Developing an
     Effective Job Security and Economic Adjustment
     Program." *Employee Relations Law Journal* 11, no. 2
     (1985): 239-68.
     Reports that U.S. employers have long viewed worker
     job security as a drag on productivity and have accepted
     layoffs as a necessary option for reversing economic
     decline. However, evidence from the recessions of the
     past decade suggests that the practice of laying off
     workers is itself costly and can seriously disrupt an
     enterprise's operations. The author presents a compre-
     hensive rationale for worker job security and describes
     various approaches for implementing job security
     programs.

80. Hansen, Gary B., and Marion T. Bentley. *Problems and
     Solutions in a Plant Shutdown: A Handbook for
     Community Involvement*. Logan, Utah: Utah State
     University, Center for Productivity and Quality of
     Working Life, 1981. 388 pp.
     Is a how-to manual that briefly discusses the
     phenomenon of plant shutdowns, their nature, extent, and
     impact; then evaluates the various ways a community can
     respond. The handbook outlines some of the major prob-
     lems encountered in a community approach, discusses
     various techniques and approaches for helping displaced
     workers and for replacing economic activities. A list
     of printed, audiovisual, and other resources available
     to help communities, employees, and unions in organizing
     to cope with shutdown is included.

81. Hansen, Gary B., Marion T. Bentley, and Richard A.
     Davidson. *Hardrock Miners in a Shutdown: A Case Study
     of the Post-Layoff Experiences of Displaced Lead-Zinc-
     Silver Miners.* Monograph No. 1. Logan, Utah: Utah
     State University, Center for Productivity and Quality
     of Working Life, 1980. 98 pp.
     Attempts to (1) document the unemployment and re-
     employment problems of the displaced workers from two
     mine shutdowns, (2) determine the effectiveness of
     various job search methods employed by the workers, and
     (3) make appropriate comparisons between the displace-
     ment experiences of the miners and those experiences
     reported in previous research studies. The study deals
     with closures of two hardrock mines in Utah, which
     displaced about 500 workers.

82. Hansen, Gary B., Marion T. Bentley, Jeannie Hepworth
     Gould, and Mark H. Skidmore. *Life After Layoff: A
     Handbook for Workers in a Plant Shutdown.* Logan,
     Utah: Utah State University, Center for Productivity
     and Quality of Working Life, 1981. 166 pp.
     Is a practical handbook written for laid-off workers
     and those facing a plant shutdown. It is a job-hunting
     guide that also deals with many of the crucial aspects
     of a plant shutdown that concern the employees, includ-
     ing financial resources, transfers, family adjustment,
     and retraining. The importance of self-assessment and
     job targeting is stressed.

83. Hansen, Gary B., Marion T. Bentley, Rexanne Pond, and
     Mark H. Skidmore. *A Selective Annotated Bibliography
     on Plant Shutdowns and Related Topics.* Logan, Utah:
     Utah State University, Center for Productivity and
     Quality of Working Life, 1981. 46 pp.
     Has approximately 120 entries arranged in seven
     categories: (1) General Topics and Case Studies, (2)
     Alternatives to Shutdowns and New Approaches to Work,
     (3) Job Search and Job-Finding Activities, (4) Organized
     Community Programs and Other Forms of Assistance, (5)
     Training and Retraining, (6) Employment Problems of
     Older Workers, and (7) Audio Visual Materials.

84. Hansen, Gary B., Marion T. Bentley, and Mark H.
     Skidmore. *Plant Shutdowns, People and Communities: A
     Selected Bibliography.* Logan, Utah: Utah State
     University, Center for Productivity and Quality of
     Working Life, 1981. 81 pp.

Cites primarily case studies dealing with plant
shutdowns. Topics covered are case studies, alternatives to shutdowns and new approaches to work, job-
finding activities, organized community programs and
other forms of assistance, training and retraining, and
employment problems of older workers.

85. Hardin, Einar, and Michael E. Borus. *The Economic
    Benefits and Costs of Retraining.* Lexington, Mass.:
    D.C. Heath and Company, 1979. 235 pp.
    Contains an in-depth study of the economic benefits
    and costs of retraining. The book contains statistical
    information, charts, graphs, and equations that repre-
    sent some of the research findings. The design and
    statistical methods used in the benefit-cost analysis
    are included.

86. Harris, Candee S. "The Magnitude of Job Loss from Plant
    Closings and the Generation of Replacement Jobs: Some
    Recent Evidence." *The Annals of the American Academy
    of Political and Social Science* 475 (Summer 1984): 15-
    27.
    Examines the employment losses and job replacement
    rates from 1976 to 1982 by type of establishment and
    geographic region. Results reveal that large manufac-
    turing firms replaced jobs lost in closings at a rate of
    only nine new jobs for each ten lost. Further, the
    industries and geographic regions showing growth in new
    jobs differ markedly from those showing decline.

87. Harris, Thomas R. "Methodologies for Modeling Impacts:
    Community Service Budgets and the Use of Micro-
    computers." Paper presented at the 1983 Annual
    American Agricultural Economics Association meeting
    symposium, Modeling Community Impacts Under Economic
    Decline: Issues and Problems. Available from the
    author at the University of Nevada, Reno. 16 pp.
    Addresses the transferability of community service
    budgets to communities experiencing declines in their
    economic activity. The final section discusses the use
    of microcomputers to partially circumvent the problems
    inherent in transferring community service budgets.

88. Henry, Mark, Mark Drabenstott, and Lynn Gibson. "A
    Changing Rural America." *Economic Review (Federal
    Reserve Bank of Kansas City)* 71, no. 7 (1986): 23-41.
    Compares the recent economic performance of rural
    America with that of urban America and explores some of

the causes of the recent poor performance of the rural
economy. The authors conclude that the historic
convergence of rural and urban income seems to have
stalled and that the remaining gap will be difficult to
remove because of structural forces now at work.

89.   Henry, Mark, Mark Drabenstott, and Lynn Gibson. "Rural
        Growth Slows Down." *Rural Development Perspectives* 3,
        no. 3 (1987): 25-30.
        Points out that rural America is again undergoing
difficult and sometimes painful economic change. After
a decade of growth, rural income, population, and overall economic activity have stalled and are again lagging
behind urban trends. Most important, the rural slowdown
seems to be caused by factors other than the normal ups
and downs in the business cycle: factors like deregulation of banking and transportation, international
competition, and financial problems in U.S. agriculture.
The only nonmetropolitan counties that have continued
robust income growth since 1979 have been those
depending on retirement, government, and trade (about a
third of all rural counties).

90.   Hettinger, Kyle B. "NRLA Preemption of State and Local
        Plant Relocating Laws." *Columbia Law Review* 86
        (1986): 407-26.
        Summarizes recent state and local plant-relocation
legislation and examines whether some provisions of
these laws may be preempted by the National Labor
Relations Act. The author concludes that certain provisions of state and local legislation are preempted
because they interfere with effective administration and
implementation of federal labor law.

91.   Hite, James, and Holley Ulbrich. "Fiscal Stress in
        Rural America: Some Straws in the Wind." *American
        Journal of Agricultural Economics* 68, no. 5 (1986):
        1188-93.
        Explores the current fiscal condition of state and
local governments serving rural America. Fiscal stress
is defined as unexpected declines in tax revenues and/or
unplanned increases in expenditure demands that the tax
base cannot support.

92.   Hodge, Gerald. "The Prediction of Trade Center
        Viability in the Great Plains." *The Regional Science
        Association Papers* 15 (1965): 87-115.

Analyzes factors affecting the growth and decline of
trade centers in Saskatchewan. Data were for the years
1941 to 1961, a period during which extensive mechani-
zation occurred in agriculture. A substantial decline
in the number of trade centers was observed, and additional decreases were predicted. Small convenience
centers located within 15 miles of a larger town were
believed to be most vulnerable.

93. Hodge, Ian. *Employment Adjustments and the Economic
    Costs of Decline in a Small Rural Community: A Case
    Study in Kellogg, Idaho.* Bull. No. 629. Moscow,
    Idaho: Idaho Agricultural Experiment Station, 1984.
    18 pp.
    Seeks to identify and measure some of the costs that
    are borne by the employees and by the community when a
    major employer closes its operation. Such costs or
    losses are grouped into four categories: (1) loss of
    productive employment, (2) costs of seeking alterna-
    tives, (3) financial and psychic costs of making the
    adjustment to the change, and (4) costs of providing
    services to the redistributed population. These costs
    are estimated for closure of the Bunker Hill metal mine
    and associated smelting and refining facilities.

94. Holmes, Alexander B., Michael J. Mueller, and Mahoud
    Motavasseli. "The Impact of a Depletable Resource on
    a Rural Area." *Regional Science Perspectives* 12, no.
    1 (1982): 19-31.
    Examines the impact of oil and gas depletion in the
    western high plains region of Oklahoma. A model is
    developed to predict crude petroleum and natural gas
    production in the ten-county area. The model and
    results are part of a larger study on the Ogallala
    Aquifer.

95. Hoppe, R.A. *Economic Structure and Change in
    Persistently Low-Income Nonmetro Counties.* Rural Dev.
    Res. Rpt. 50. Washington, D.C.: USDA, Economic
    Research Service, October 1985. 25 pp.
    Discovered that some nonmetropolitan areas, largely in
    the South, remained as severely depressed during the
    seventies as they had been for decades, despite non-
    metropolitan America's general economic gains during the
    period. These counties differed from other nonmetro-
    politan counties in location, population character-
    istics, economic structure, and farm structure. How-
    ever, some severely depressed counties improved their

incomes in the seventies, primarily through nonfarm
industries such as services and manufacturing. Mining
also provided a large share of the growth in some of the
counties with the largest income improvements. Some
counties that escaped from low-income status earlier in
the decade returned to low-income status by 1979.

96. Howell, Robert E., and Marion T. Bentley. *Assessing,*
     Managing, and Mitigating the Impacts of Economic
     Decline: A Community Perspective. WREP 91.
     Corvallis, Ore.: Oregon State University, Western
     Rural Development Center, 1986. 11 pp.
     Presents a model for guiding impact assessment of a
     substantial reduction in employment due to plant
     closures and layoffs and for management and mitigation
     activities for local communities. The paper provides a
     framework around which the Communities in Transition
     project (developed in thirteen western states) was
     organized.

97. Ilbery, Brian W. "Harvey's Principles Reapplied: A Case
     Study of the Declining West Midland Hop Industry."
     Geoforum 14, no. 1 (1983): 111-23.
     Applies the principles developed by Harvey to a
     declining rather than expanding industry. The role of
     distance as a locational factor is examined and shown to
     be of continuing importance as the industry becomes
     increasingly concentrated around a core parish. Ilbery
     concludes that Harvey's principles are of limited value
     when attempting to explain patterns of decline. Rather,
     the complexity of the situation and the decision-making
     processes of the hop growers need to be examined.

98. Jenkins, Glenn P., and Claude Montmarquette.
     "Estimating the Private and Social Opportunity Cost of
     Displaced Workers." *The Review of Economics and*
     Statistics 6, no. 3 (August 1979): 342-53.
     Outlines a framework for estimating the opportunity
     cost of workers who are permanently displaced from their
     previous place of employment. The framework is applied
     to an empirical estimation of the private and social
     opportunity cost of labor and the adjustment costs
     associated with workers laid off by the aircraft indus-
     try in Canada. Results indicate that both of these
     measures of adjustment costs were greatly affected by
     the age distribution of the displaced work force and the
     rate of regional unemployment and that the critical
     determinant of social costs of displaced labor from a

declining firm is the amount of other subsidies and
protection received by the firm.

* Johansen, Harley E., and Glenn V. Fuguitt. "Population
    Growth and Retail Decline: Conflicting Effects of
    Urban Accessibility in American Villages." Cited
    above as item 12.

99.   Johnson, Bruce, and Joel Young. *Trends in Retail Sales
      Activity Across Nebraska's Counties and Communities.*
      Lincoln, Nebr.: University of Nebraska, Department of
      Agricultural Economics, 1987. 31 pp.
      Traces patterns of retail trade activity in Nebraska
      since 1970. The analysis focuses on the more agricul-
      tural counties and smaller rural communities, assesses
      their relative performance, and discusses possible
      causes and implications.

100. Johnson, Kenneth M. "Organizational Adjustment to
      Population Change in Nonmetropolitan America: A
      Longitudinal Analysis of Retail Trade." *Social Forces*
      60, no. 4 (1982): 1123-39.
      Examines the impact of population change on retailing
      using longitudinal data from nonmetropolitan counties.
      The response to population change included shifts in
      both the number and operational scale of units. Adjust-
      ments in the number of establishments were in the same
      direction as, but less than proportionate to, population
      shifts. The retail response to population increase was
      not symmetrical to that for decline, indicating that the
      hypothesis that a single process of organization adjust-
      ment could accommodate both growth and decline should be
      rejected.

101. Kinicki, Angelo J. "Personal Consequences of Plant
      Closings: A Model and Preliminary Test." *Human
      Relations* 38, no. 3 (March 1985): 197-212.
      Proposes a model that specifies affective response to
      plant closings. Results of a survey of 60 individuals
      who had been out of work an average of 119 days indicate
      that employability had a direct effect on employment
      status; employment was associated with having more
      education, being younger, and being male. In addition,
      workers who have a premonition about a future closing
      may be able to devise coping mechanisms to reduce the
      frequency of stressful life events. Employment status,
      work orientation, and stressful life events all had a
      direct effect on total individual costs.

102. Kovach, Kenneth A., and Peter E. Millspaugh. "Plant
      Closings: Is the American Industrial Relations System
      Failing?" *Business Horizons* 30 (March 1980): 44-49.
      Analyzes the role of the National Labor Relations
      Board, the Supreme Court, the U.S. Congress, and labor-
      management collective bargaining in accommodating the
      anticipated, sustained pattern of business closings.

103. Kuehn, John A., and Curtis H. Braschler. *Impacts of
      Foreign Trade, Automation, and Comparative Advantage
      on Manufacturing Employment Changes, 1975-80.* ERS
      Staff Report No. AGES 850730. Washington, D.C.: USDA,
      Economic Research Service, October 1985. 19 pp.
      Uses a modified shift-share analysis for 1975-1980 to
      produce the following results: (1) 122,000 total net
      manufacturing jobs were lost to foreign trade; (2) auto-
      mation accounted for about 1.8 million job losses; (3)
      apparel, leather, and motor vehicle industries lost many
      jobs to foreign trade; (4) the Great Lakes region lost
      many jobs to the South Atlantic, Southwest, and Far West
      regions; and (5) gains in nonmetropolitan areas were
      mainly in low-growth industries.

104. Leistritz, F. Larry, Holly E. Bastow-Shoop, and Brenda
      L. Ekstrom. "How Small Businesses in North Dakota
      Towns Adjust to Regional Economic Decline." *Small
      Town* 17, no. 6 (May-June 1987): 4-13.
      Examines selected characteristics of main street
      businesses in six of North Dakota's nonmetropolitan
      trade centers. Specific aspects examined include the
      customer base, business income and net worth, managerial
      adjustments, and the economic outlook of business pro-
      prietors. Altogether, 547 businesses and 68 former
      businesses participated in the survey.

105. Leistritz, F. Larry, and Brenda L. Ekstrom.
      *Interdependencies of Agriculture and Rural
      Communities: An Annotated Bibliography.* New York:
      Garland Publishing, 1986. 200 pp.
      Contains nearly 600 items on socioeconomic changes in
      rural communities, the role of shifts in agricultural
      structure and technology in stimulating such changes,
      and the role of the local economy in influencing farm
      organization and the life-styles of farm families. Many
      of the annotated works review the economic, demographic,
      public service, fiscal, and social changes in rural
      communities over the past several decades and describe
      the effects of the current economic crisis in agricul-

ture on farm families, agribusiness, and rural communities.

106. Leistritz, F. Larry, and Brenda L. Ekstrom. *Social Impact Assessment and Management: An Annotated Bibliography.* New York: Garland Publishing, 1986. 343 pp.
Contains over 1,000 annotated entries on social impact assessment and mitigation. The literature examines social and economic effects of policies, programs, and projects; discusses alternative methods for anticipating these effects; and describes measures to ameliorate impacts that are deemed undesirable and/or to accentuate effects deemed beneficial.

107. Leistritz, F. Larry, Brenda L. Ekstrom, and Harvey G. Vreugdenhil. *Causes and Consequences of Economic Stress in Agriculture: Contrasting the Views of Rural Residents.* Agr. Econ. Rpt. 219. Fargo, N. Dak.: North Dakota Agr. Exp. Sta., Dept. Agr. Econ., 1987. 42 pp.
Contrasts and compares the views of over 900 current and former farmers, over 600 current and former business operators, and over 500 community residents regarding their opinions of the causes and community consequences of current farm financial conditions.

108. Leistritz, F. Larry, Brenda L. Ekstrom, and Harvey G. Vreugdenhil. *Selected Characteristics of Business Operators in North Dakota Agricultural Trade Centers.* Agr. Econ. Rpt. 217. Fargo, N. Dak.: North Dakota Agr. Exp. Sta., Dept. Agr. Econ., 1987. 62 pp.
Examines the adjustment problems (as a result of the current farm financial crisis) encountered by business operators and former business operators in six rural North Dakota communities. Financial characteristics of the business operation are examined along with demographic characteristics of the operators, their personal financial characteristics and trade patterns, their level of community participation, and their attitudes and perceptions concerning local business conditions. Altogether, 547 business operators and 68 former business operators were surveyed.

109. Leistritz, F. Larry, Brenda L. Ekstrom, Janet Wanzek, and Harvey G. Vreugdenhil. *Selected Socioeconomic Characteristics of North Dakota Community Residents.*

Agr. Econ. Rpt. 218. Fargo, N. Dak.: North Dakota
Agr. Exp. Sta., Dept. Agr. Econ., 1987. 34 pp.
Examines the following characteristics of over 500
residents of rural North Dakota communities: demographic characteristics, employment history and
vocational skills, financial characteristics, trade
patterns, and community participation. The study was
conducted to determine the response of rural residents
to current farm financial conditions.

110. Lichter, Daniel T. "Measuring Underemployment in Rural
     Areas." *Rural Development Perspectives* 3, no. 1
     (1987): 11-14.
     Defines the underemployed as those who are unemployed,
     working for low pay, or working too few hours. The
     author points out that nearly one-third of the rural
     labor force is underemployed, using this definition, but
     only about one-third of these are currently reflected in
     unemployment statistics.

111. Little, Craig B. "Technical-Professional Unemployment:
     Middle-class Adaptability to Personal Crisis." *The
     Sociological Quarterly* 17 (Spring 1976): 262-74.
     Reveals that, for many of the 100 unemployed male
     technical-professional workers of the aerospace-defense-
     electronics industry, unemployment was less stressful
     than expected. Many viewed the unemployment as an
     opportunity to seek more desirable employment. Factors
     directly related to the unemployed worker's financial
     situation are most important as predictors of their
     reactions to unemployment.

112. McKersie, Robert B., and Werner Sengenberger. *Job
     Losses in Major Industries*. Paris: Organization for
     Economic Cooperation and Development (OECD), 1983.
     125 pp.
     Deals with large-scale dislocations of industrial
     employment in a number of OECD countries, and describes
     their significance and the consequences (economic and
     other) for the workers, communities, and regions
     affected. It also discusses the structural changes that
     have led up to these situations, and the range of
     national and industrial strategies applied to respond to
     them. Much of the report is devoted to a detailed
     analysis of integrative strategies and conversion pro-
     grams that seek to reconcile capital mobility with labor
     protection.

113. MacKinnon, David A. "Military Base Closures: Long Range
     Economic Effects and the Implications for Industrial
     Development." *American Industrial Development Council
     Journal* 13, no. 3 (1978): 7-41.
     Explores the economic climate of seven communities,
     each of which had an Air Force base that closed in the
     mid 1960s, to determine what the actual long-term eco-
     nomic impact has been. A topic of special interest was
     to determine what implications these base closures have
     had for local industrial development.

114. McManis Associates, Inc. *Coping with the Loss of a
     Major Employer: A How-To Manual.* Washington, D.C.:
     U.S. Department of Commerce, Economic Development
     Administration, n.d. 40 pp.
     Offers a four-step process that community leaders and
     government officials can use for developing and execut-
     ing a strategy to adjust to a major employer's unex-
     pected announcement to close or severely reduce
     operations in a local facility. The steps include
     organizing, analyzing the cause of dislocation and
     adjustment options, developing a strategy to undertake
     the selected options, and executing the strategy.

115. Martin, R.L. "Job Loss and the Regional Incidence of
     Redundancies in the Current Recession." *Cambridge
     Journal of Economics* 6 (December 1982): 375-95.
     Analyzes regional incidence of job loss in Great
     Britain over the period 1978-1981, by examining first
     the geography of mass redundancy and the influence of
     industrial structure, and then the regional patterns of
     recession in terms of net job loss. Martin then com-
     ments on potential future problems.

116. Martinez, Doug. "The Boom Has Faded, and Many Rural
     Areas Lag Behind." *Farmline* 6, no. 3 (April 1985):
     12-13.
     Draws comparisons between regional employment growth
     and between rural and urban employment growth in various
     economic sectors from 1940 to the present.

117. Mick, Stephen S. "Social and Personal Costs of Plant
     Shutdowns." *Industrial Relations* 14, no. 2 (May
     1975): 203-8.
     Introduces the reader to the subject of plant shut-
     downs and the problems arising from them. Three areas
     are discussed: a definition of a plant shutdown, a
     review of literature about the effects of shutdowns on

employees, and an analysis of a plant shutdown in one
industry over a sixteen-year period.

118. Murdock, Steve H., and F. Larry Leistritz, eds. *The
     Farm Financial Crisis: Socioeconomic Dimensions and
     Implications for Producers and Rural Areas.* Boulder,
     Colo.: Westview Press, 1988. 250 pp.
     Analyzes the socioeconomic context, impacts, and long-
     term consequences of the farm financial crisis of the
     1980s in relation to how they affect current and former
     farm and ranch operators, current and former business
     operators, employees of rural businesses, and other
     rural residents in agriculturally dependent rural areas
     in the United States. The book closes with a discussion
     of implications and policy alternatives.
     Contains items 17 and 120.

119. Murdock, Steve H., F. Larry Leistritz, Rita R. Hamm, Don
     E. Albrecht, and Arlen G. Leholm. "Impacts of the
     Farm Crisis on a Rural Community." *Journal of the
     Community Development Society* 18, no. 1 (1987): 30-49.
     Points out that, while the farm crisis is affecting
     many sectors of rural society, few empirical analyses of
     the impacts of the crisis on rural communities have been
     completed. A case study of a rural community was con-
     ducted using informal interviews with community leaders
     as well as formal interviews of current and former busi-
     ness operators and community residents.

120. Murdock, Steve H., Lloyd Potter, Rita R. Hamm, Kenneth
     Backman, and Don E. Albrecht. "The Implications of
     the Current Farm Crisis for Rural America." *The Farm
     Financial Crisis: Socioeconomic Dimensions and Impli-
     cations for Producers and Rural Areas* (item 118).
     Examines the implications of the loss of alternative
     numbers of residents from agriculturally dependent rural
     areas in the United States. Specifically examined are
     the quantitative effects on the structure of agriculture
     and on the economic, demographic, public service, and
     fiscal characteristics of these areas and the
     qualitative effects on the social structure of rural
     areas.

121. Parnes, Herbert S., and Randy King. "Middle-aged Job
     Losers." *Industrial Gerontology* 4 (Spring 1977): 77-
     95.
     Uses national longitudinal data to analyze the
     experiences of unemployed men over age 45. Workers

displaced in 1966 had occupational and educational
characteristics similar to employed workers. The major
long-term impact appears to have been a substantial
deterioration in occupational status. In addition to
economic losses, many displaced workers also suffered
from deteriorating health and in some cases from a sense
of alienation.

122. Paulsen, Arnold, and Jerry Carlson. "Is Rural Main
       Street Disappearing?" *Change in Rural America:
       Causes, Consequences, and Alternatives.* St. Louis,
       Mo.: C.V. Mosby Co., 1978. pp. 64-65.
       Points out the effects of farm consolidation on main
       street businesses in rural towns. Consolidation will
       have differential effects on different types of busi-
       nesses. Consumer-goods businesses are most affected by
       changes in net farm income and in the number of farmers
       in the area. Production-goods businesses are most
       sensitive to changes in the volume of production and
       hence in the level of expenditures for production
       inputs. Finally, firms engaged in handling, trans-
       porting, and processing farm products are most affected
       by changes in the physical volume of farm output.

123. Penson, John B., Jr., and Murray E. Fulton. "Impact of
       Localized Cutbacks in Agricultural Production on a
       State Economy." *Western Journal of Agricultural
       Economics* 5, no. 2 (1980): 107-22.
       Examines the effects that a cutback in production by
       Texas agricultural producers would have on the economic
       well-being of all producers and consumers in the state's
       economy. A quadratic input-output model incorporating
       econometric estimates of final demand was developed.

124. Perkins, Marianna M. "Economically Motivated Partial
       Closings: The Duty of Management to Decision-Bargain."
       Labor Law Journal 31, no. 11 (November 1980): 700-8.
       Analyzes an employer's responsibility for a partial
       closing motivated solely by economic considerations.

125. Preissing, John F., and Jerry Robert Skees. "Problems
       with Unemployment Statistics for Rural Areas." Paper
       presented at the annual meeting of the American Agri-
       cultural Economics Association, Michigan State Univer-
       sity, August 2-5, 1987. 14 pp. Available from the
       senior author at the University of Kentucky, Dept.
       Agr. Econ.

Addresses the problems of using unemployment statistics in nonmetropolitan areas. Conceptual problems and
problems of measurement in compiling reliable unemployment measures are reviewed. Results of a survey are
compared with official estimates for the same area and
suggest that official figures may seriously under-
estimate unemployment in rural areas.

126. Raines, John C., Lenora E. Berson, and David McI.
      Gracie, eds. *Community and Capital in Conflict: Plant
      Closings and Job Loss*. Philadelphia: Temple
      University Press, 1982. 318 pp.
      Centers on the movement of jobs and capital from
      Philadelphia, the Northeast, and the country. Various
      authors discuss the ethical and economic aspects of
      plant closings and job loss; they examine the deterio-
      ration of neighborhoods, housing and services, and
      family life.

127. Raup, Philip M. "Economic Aspects of Population Decline
      in Rural Communities." *Labor Mobility and Population
      in Agriculture*. Ames, Iowa: Iowa State University
      Press, 1961. pp. 95-106.
      Delineates the changes in rural communities brought
      about by the truck transport revolution and examines the
      nature of the changing configuration of rural villages
      in American agriculture, the reasons that have brought
      it about, and some of the private and public costs
      associated with the change.

128. Root, Kenneth. *Companies, Mines and Factories--
      Shutdowns, Closures and Moves: A Bibliography*.
      Monticello, Illinois: Vance Bibliographies, 1979.   23
      pp.
      Contains about 250 entries on plant shutdowns and
      relocations, and related social changes, family crises,
      and agency programs. Literature relates mainly to the
      United States and to current research, although some
      classic and descriptive works date back to the 1930s.

129. Root, Kenneth A. *Assistance to Dislocated Farmers:
      Alternatives of Acceptable Help*. Ames, Iowa: North
      Central Regional Center for Rural Development, Iowa
      State University, 1986. 43 pp.
      Uses data from a survey of 192 operating farmers in
      the Midwest, 11 dislocated Iowa farmers, and 103 workers
      unemployed due to the closure of the Armour plant in
      Mason City, Iowa. The study sought to discover where

workers would (or did) seek help, whether the problems facing currently displaced workers differ from those of workers during the Depression, and what happens to farmers in difficulty who have to seek a new job, a new home, and new way of life.

130. Rose, David, Carolyn Vogler, Gordon Marshall, and Howard Newby. "Economic Restructuring: The British Experience." *The Annals of the American Academy of Political and Social Science* 475 (September 1984): 137-57.
    Presents a brief historical review of British economic performance, then examines the phenomenon of deindustrialization. Two economic theories are discussed, and the effects of multinational firms are briefly examined. Finally, the social and political aspects of deindustrialization are examined.

131. Rothstein, Lawrence E. *Plant Closings: Power, Politics, and Workers*. Dover, Mass.: Auburn House Publishing, 1986. 201 pp.
    Seeks to dispell myths about big labor, the business climate, and legality as it relates to plant-closing legislation. Rothstein offers suggestions to the U.S. labor movement on overcoming the present decline of trade unionism and on improving the promotion of workers' interests. He also reviews the different historical and ideological backgrounds of European and American labor movements.

132. Rowthorn, Bob, and Terry Ward. "How to Run a Company and Run Down an Economy: The Effects of Closing Down Steel-Making in Corby." *Cambridge Journal of Economics* 3 (1979): 327-40.
    Attempts to quantify the overall economic implications of the British Steel Corporation's plan to close down an iron- and steel-making plant at Corby in Northamptonshire. The more general purpose is to argue that projects should not be evaluated solely in the narrow commercial criterion of profit and loss to the firm in question but rather that, in comparing various alternatives, their macroeconomic implications should be taken explicitly into account.

133. Sattler, Edward L., and Robert C. Scott. "Price and Output Adjustments in the Two-Plant Firm." *Southern Economic Journal* 48, no. 4 (April 1982): 1042-48.

Raises questions about the behavior of multiplant
firms. For a profit-maximizing firm, the shutdown of
one plant may cause increased output from an operating
plant, the firm's marginal cost curve will be discon-
tinuous at the point of shutdown of one plant, and a
decline in demand may cause a rise in price.

134. Schlottmann, Alan M., and Henry W. Herzog, Jr.
      "Employment Status and the Decision to Migrate."
      Review of Economics and Statistics 63, no. 4 (1981):
      590-98.
      Uses econometric analysis of the 1965-1970 interstate
      behavior of employed and unemployed persons to examine
      the demographic and socioeconomic determinants of
      migration.

135. Schweke, William, and David R. Jones. "European Job
      Creation in the Wake of Plant Closing and Layoffs."
      Monthly Labor Review 109 (October 1986): 18-22.
      Examines efforts by France, Italy, and Great Britain
      to stimulate job creation and new business growth in the
      wake of a plant closing or major layoff. The authors
      provide an introduction to development tools (such as
      incubators, technical and financial assistance, and
      entrepreneurial training) American leaders could use to
      ameliorate the effects of economic dislocation.

136. Scott, M.J., D.B. Belzer, R.J. Nesse, R.W. Schultz, P.A.
      Stokowski, and D.C. Clark. *The Economic and Community
      Impacts of Closing Hanford's N Reactor and Nuclear
      Materials Production Facilities.* PNL-6295. Richland,
      Wash.: Battelle Pacific Northwest Laboratory, 1987.
      90 pp.
      Discusses the negative economic impact on local cities
      and counties and the state of Washington of a permanent
      closure of nuclear materials production at the Hanford
      Site. The loss of nuclear materials production, the
      largest and most important of the five Department of
      Energy missions at Hanford, could occur if Hanford's N
      Reactor is permanently closed and not replaced. The
      study provides estimates of statewide and local losses
      in jobs, income, and purchases from the private sector
      caused by such an event; it forecasts impacts on state
      and local government finances; and it describes certain
      local community and social impacts in the Tri-Cities
      (Richland, Kennewick, and Pasco) and surrounding commu-
      nities.

137. Sewel, John, and Peter Wybrow. *Invergordon Smelter
      Project: Preliminary Research Report.* ISO1. Aber-
      deen, Scotland: University of Aberdeen, Institute for
      the Study of Sparsely Populated Areas, 1982. 37 pp.
      Reports on the impacts of the closure of the Inver-
      gordon Smelter in Easter Ross, Scotland. The smelter,
      which had begun operations in 1968, employed about 890
      persons. Six months after closure only 7 percent had
      migrated out of Easter Ross, but only 23 percent had
      been successful in finding full-time permanent
      employment, and 53 percent were without any form of
      work. The authors also discuss changes in workers'
      financial circumstances and future plans.

138. Sheehan, Michael F. "Plant Closings and the Community:
      The Instrumental Value of Public Enterprise in
      Countering Corporate Flight." *American Journal of
      Economics and Sociology* 44, no. 4 (1985): 423-33.
      Reports that over the last ten years, ten million jobs
      have been lost and millions of dollars in capital
      rendered unproductive from plant closings in New England
      and the Upper Midwest. Some were weeded out by the
      discipline of the market, but the author feels that most
      were moving to cut labor costs and claim subsidies from
      governments seeking to expand local job opportunities,
      and some were using the threat of closing to exact
      concessions from labor and government. In some cases it
      is possible for municipal governments to buy or condemn
      the plant and operate it as a public enterprise; muni-
      cipal operation is often more efficient and productive.
      Municipally owned and operated public enterprise should
      command serious consideration as an option like cooper-
      ative ownership.

139. Sheppard, Harold L. *New Perspectives on Older Workers.*
      Kalamazoo, Mich.: W.E. Upjohn Institute for Employment
      Research, 1971. 90 pp.
      Discusses the status of older Americans in the job
      market, age and migration factors in the socioeconomic
      conditions of urban black and white women, the emerging
      pattern of second careers, and the potential role of
      behavioral science in the solution of the "older worker
      problem."

140. Simon, William, and John H. Gagnon. "The Decline and
      Fall of the Small Town." *The Community: A Comparative
      Perspective.* Edited by Robert Mills French. Itasca,
      Ill.: F.E. Peacock Publishers, 1969. pp. 497-510.

Presents a detailed analysis of three neighboring
rural towns in southern Illinois to determine why,
despite many similarities in location, economic
problems, and history, they developed differently after
World War II. The area has been dependent largely on
the coal industry, and declining mining activity forced
all three towns to seek means to strengthen and diver-
sify their economic base.

141. Smith, I.J., and M.J. Taylor. "Takeover, Closures, and
      the Restructuring of the Ironfoundry Industry."
      Environment and Planning A 15 (1983): 639-61.
      Explores the regional dimension of plant and firm
      closure in the United Kingdom using data for the
      ironfoundry industry over the postwar period with
      particular emphasis on 1967 to 1980. Impact of owner-
      ship on plant closure is stressed, and patterns of
      ownership change are shown to seriously prejudice the
      survival of plants in the United Kingdom's peripheral
      regions.

142. Staudohar, Paul D., and Holly E. Brown. *Deindus-
      trialization and Plant Closure.* Lexington, Mass.:
      Lexington Books, 1987. 348 pp.
      Presents a collection of twenty-six readings that
      focus on the debate over deindustrialization and plant
      closure. It raises crucial questions that frame this
      debate and seeks to provide answers that can be trans-
      lated into policy development. The work is organized
      into five major sections: (1) overview; (2) impact of
      plant closure; (3) management, union, and public
      policies; (4) perspectives from foreign counties; and
      (5) state laws and proposed federal legislation.

143. Stern, James L. "Consequences of Plant Closure." *The
      Journal of Human Resources* 7, no. 1 (1972): 3-25.
      Uses pre- and postshutdown annual earnings reported to
      the Social Security Administration to measure the
      economic impact of plant closure on the income of
      workers exercising different vocational choices.
      Workers who sought new jobs in the local labor market
      suffered substantial reductions in postshutdown annual
      earnings. With the influence of age, skill, sex,
      seniority, education, race, and preshutdown earnings
      held constant, short-term training did not improve the
      situation significantly. Workers who elected the
      interplant transfer option increased their annual
      earnings by more than $2,000.

144. Stone, Kenneth E. "Impact of the Farm Financial Crisis on the Retail and Service Sectors of Rural Communities." *Agricultural Finance Review* 47 (1987): 40-47. Shows the effects of the continuing loss of economic base in rural areas caused by technology displacing farmers. Trends in retail sales for various-sized towns, effects on farm-related firms, and the spending psychology among consumers are discussed. The article closes with a discussion of the future of rural communities.

145. Stucker, James P., Charles L. Batten, Kenneth A. Solomon, and Werner Z. Hirsch. *Costs of Closing the Indian Point Nuclear Power Plant*. R-2857-NYO. Santa Monica, Calif.: RAND Corporation, 1981. 85 pp. Estimates the monetary costs that would result from closing the nuclear power generating facilities at Indian Point, New York. The report estimates the total magnitude of the costs, the major components of cost, and the sensitivity of those components to major underlying assumptions.

146. Swanson, Larry Douglas. "A Study in Socioeconomic Development: Changing Farm Structure and Rural Community Decline in the Context of the Technological Transformation of U.S. Agriculture." Ph.D. Dissertation. Lincoln: University of Nebraska, 1980. 319 pp. Evaluates the extent to which important elements of rural community structure in an agricultural region of Nebraska are differentiated according to key components of the area's farm structure. The author argues that the viability of rural, agricultural communities is to a large degree a function of, or derived from, the nature of the area's farm structure. Data from twenty-seven rural counties for the period 1940-1974 were analyzed.

147. U.S. Congress, House. *Worker Dislocation, Capital Flight and Plant Closings*. Hearings before the Subcommittee on Labor-Management Relations, under the Committee on Education and Labor. Washington, D.C.: Government Printing Office, 1984. 454 pp. Contains statements on the topic by community and labor leaders, government officials, unemployed workers, and corporate executives.

148. U.S. Congress, Senate. *Governing the Heartland: Can Rural Communities Survive the Farm Crisis?* Prepared

by the Subcommittee on Intergovernmental Relations of
the Committee on Governmental Affairs. Washington,
D.C.: May 1986 (draft). 56 pp.

Documents the problems of rural community officials
faced with a declining revenue base. The report
examines the agricultural economy of the eighties, the
estimated property tax impacts in agriculturally dependent counties, local government expenditures and future
impacts on it, long-term effects on communities, and
policy options.

149. U.S. Congress, Senate. *Too Old to Work--Too Young to
Retire: A Case Study of a Permanent Plant Shutdown.*
Washington, D.C.: Government Printing Office, 1960.
74 pp. (Doc. Y4.Un23: Sh9)

Reports findings of a research project about the
effects of a 1956 permanent plant shutdown on 500 former
employees of Packard Motor Company in Detroit. Issues
discussed are shutdown notification; job search;
workers' expectations of the government, the union, and
management; and the social psychological impact of
length of unemployment.

150. U.S. Department of Labor, Employment and Training
Administration. *Employment-Related Problems of Older
Workers: A Research Strategy.* R&D Monograph 73.
Washington, D.C.: Government Printing Office, 1979.
138 pp. (Doc. L37.14: 73)

Assesses available literature on older workers and
their job-related problems and examines demographic
changes likely to influence the size and characteristics
of the older worker population in the 1980s and 1990s.
Other topics include health, safety, and aging in the
workplace; job performance and training of older workers; and part-time work and tapered retirement. Separate sections discuss older working women, older
minority group workers, and older workers in rural
areas.

151. Udis, Bernard, ed. *The Economic Consequences of Reduced
Military Spending.* Lexington, Mass.: Lexington Books,
1973. 398 pp.

Reviews the likely economic impact of reduced military
expenditures on the economy of the United States and
identifies some of the more pressing problems, which may
be encountered in the shift of resources from military
to nonmilitary uses.

Contains items 55, 57, and 58.

152. Weeks, Edward C. *Plant Modernization and Community Economic Stability: Managing the Transition.* Eugene, Ore.: University of Oregon, Bureau of Governmental Research and Service, 1983. 77 pp.
Traces the connections between current economic forces, plant modernization, and mill closures in Oregon's forestry industry and examines some of the socioeconomic consequences of mill closures in small communities. The final section reviews a variety of policies offered as solutions to the problem of plant closure.

153. Western Analysis. *An Economic and Social Assessment of the Anaconda Company Smelter Closure: Anaconda, Montana.* Helena, Mont.: Western Analysis, 1981. 58 pp.
Describes the economic and social conditions in Anaconda prior to the smelter closure and assesses the impact of the shutdown on the community.

154. Williams, Anne S. "Leadership Patterns in the Declining Rural Community." *Journal of Community Development Society* 5, no. 2 (1974): 98-106.
Reviews the literature on leadership patterns in declining rural communities and offers two suggestions for improvement: leadership training and redefining the boundaries of rural organizational units (counties) into larger multicounty areas that could more efficiently provide administrative and public services.

155. Young, John A., and Jan M. Newton. *Capitalism and Human Obsolescence.* New York: Universe Books, 1980. 253 pp.
Focuses on the causes and consequences of economic decline and unemployment in rural, single-industry communities. The authors present economic analyses of the Oregon lumber industry, Hawaiian plantation agriculture, copper mining in Arizona, small-scale farming in California, and small business in an economically declining region in Washington.

Policies and Issues

156. Aboud, Antone, ed. *Plant Closing Legislation.* Key Issues No. 27. Ithaca, N.Y.: ILR Press, Cornell University, New York State School of Industrial and Labor Relations, 1984. 60 pp.

Discusses the laws and reality of plant closings in
Maine, overviews legislation and issues, provides a
conceptual framework for controlling plant closings, and
reviews obligations under the National Labor Relations
Act.

157. Alexander, James R. "Policy Design and the Impact of
      Federal Aid to Declining Communities." *Growth and
      Change* 12 (January 1981): 35-41.
      Reviews federal policies that are designed to address
the needs of declining communities. Alexander differen-
tiates three types of community needs: social, economic, and fiscal. The author assesses the impacts that
the design and implementation of federal policies have
on the types of needs exhibited by declining communities.

158. Bendick, Marc, and Larry C. Ledebur. "National Indus-
      trial Policy and Economically Distressed Communities."
      Policy Studies Journal 10, no. 2 (1981): 220-34.
      Presents empirical evidence that policies designed to
affect the growth or decline of firms or industries for
the sake of aggregate national prosperity and international competitiveness would be targeted differently
from those designed to promote development of economically distressed regions and communities.

159. Berenbeim, Ronald E. *Company Programs to Ease the
      Impact of Shutdowns*. Rpt. No. 878. New York: The
      Conference Board, 1986. 57 pp.
      Relates the results of a survey of 512 human-resource
vice presidents about company policies and practices on
facility closures. Surveys were also sent to Job Training Partnership coordinators in fifty states to obtain
an overview of state practices. Six case studies are
also included.

160. Brown, A.J., and E.M. Burrows. *Regional Economic
      Problems: Comparative Experiences of Some Market
      Economies*. London: George Allen & Unwin, Ltd., 1977.
      209 pp.
      Discusses, first, the basis for having a regional
policy, then describes major types of problem regions.
The authors then examine four of the common types of
problem areas in detail: agricultural, coal-mining, old
manufacturing, and congestion areas. The book closes
with an examination of the methods and effectiveness of
regional policies.

161. Cook, James. "The Argument for Plant-Closing Legis-
     lation: An Interview with Economist Barry Bluestone."
     Forbes 131, no. 13 (June 20, 1983): 82-84.
     Presents an interview with Bluestone on such topics as
     the growing antagonism between labor and management,
     regulation of industrial mergers and acquisition, plan-
     ning the velocity of capital movement, and plant-
     closing legislation.

 *   Cumberland, John H. "Dimensions of the Impact of
     Reduced Military Expenditures on Industries, Regions,
     and Communities." Cited above as item 55.

 *   Erickson, Jon. *Plant Closings: Impact, Causes, and
     Policies.* Cited above as item 68.

162. Folbre, Nance R., Julia L. Leighton, and Melissa R.
     Roderick. "Plant Closings and Their Regulation in
     Maine, 1971-1982." *Industrial and Labor Relations
     Review* 37, no. 2 (January 1984): 185-96.
     Describes plant closing regulations adopted in Maine
     during the 1971-1981 period and documents a pattern of
     relatively poor compliance with the prenotification and
     severance pay requirements of the law. Data on the
     number of workers laid off in major plant closings, on
     prenotification of workers, and on state and local
     unemployment rates provide the basis for an econometric
     estimate of the effects of closings with and without
     early notification on local unemployment rates and the
     size of the local labor force. The results indicate
     that prenotification significantly lowers the unemploy-
     ment resulting from a closing.

163. Gilford, Dorothy M., Glenn L. Nelson, and Linda Ingram,
     eds. *Rural America in Passage: Statistics for Policy.*
     Washington, D.C.: National Academy Press, 1981. 592
     pp.
     Assesses the quality and availability of data for
     rural development policy by attempting to define *rural*
     and *development*; identifying various data needs of
     different levels of rural development policymakers,
     analysts, and administrators; and discussing specific
     data elements and procedures organized by development
     goals.

 *   Gordus, Jeanne P., Paul Jarley, and Louis A. Ferman.
     Plant Closing and Economic Dislocation. Cited above
     as item 75.

164. Halstead, John M., Robert A. Chase, and F. Larry
      Leistritz. *Mitigating Impacts of Plant Closures: A
      Survey of the Issues.* AE 83008. Fargo, N. Dak.:
      North Dakota State University, Dept. Agr. Econ., July
      1983. 17 pp.
      Attempts to survey some of the key impacts and issues
      of plant closings and alternatives for communities
      facing mass layoffs. The report describes the risk
      factors in industrial development and the consequences
      of closure, presents case studies of the Colony oil
      shale project in Colorado and the Anaconda Company's
      copper operations in Montana, reviews some proposed
      plant closure legislation, and discusses community
      alternatives.

165. Harrison, Bennett. "The International Movement for
      Prenotification of Plant Closures." *Industrial
      Relations* 23, no. 3 (Fall 1984): 387-409.
      First, reviews the incidence of industrial plant
      shutdowns and the granting of advance notice in the
      United States and Western Europe, then places the
      differences in the context of their different traditions
      of labor law.

166. Harrison, Bennett, and Barry Bluestone. "The Incidence
      and Regulation of Plant Shutdowns." *Policy Studies
      Journal* 10, no. 2 (1981): 297-320.
      Examines the development of expanding support for
      worker ownership in the United States. Related
      legislation is reviewed, and problems in establishing
      and maintaining a worker-owned firm are discussed.

167. Hearn, Frank, Michael Mertens, and Jamie Faricellia.
      "An American Tragedy: Act Two." *Dissent* 30 (Spring
      1983): 183-89.
      Documents the 1982 announcement of the closure of the
      Smith-Corona typewriter plant in Cortland, New York, and
      the community efforts prior to 1982 to pressure local
      politicians to take responsibility in meeting the crisis
      faced by a community encountering major job losses. The
      citizens organized their efforts around the issue of
      prenotification of workers of impending closure of
      plants employing more than 500 workers. Although the
      legislation was opposed by the mayor, chamber of com-
      merce, and business leaders, the group's initial support
      and growing publicity pressured the employer to act more
      responsibly by giving workers eighteen months' notice.

168. Hegadoren, D.B., and J.C. Day. "Socioeconomic Mine
      Termination Policies: A Case Study of Mine Closure in
      Ontario." *Resources Policy* 7, no. 4 (December 1981):
      265-72.
      Discusses the inevitable socioeconomic changes induced
      by mine closure. The article documents and evaluates
      the public and private sector's arrangements to
      ameliorate closure impacts at the Marmoraton mining
      facility in Ontario during 1978. Measures used to
      reduce detrimental hardships of mine terminations on
      Canadian communities are presented. Such recommended
      measures include an ex ante economic impact analysis of
      mine termination, local-hiring policy, termination
      benefits for workers, and government-financed economic
      feasibility studies.

169. Hekman, John S., and John S. Strong. "Is There a Case
      for Plant Closing Laws?" *New England Economic Review*
      (July-August 1980): 34-51.
      Describes and analyzes both sides of the debate over
      plant-closing laws and attempts to clarify the many
      issues involved. As one way of illustrating the
      possible policies toward plant closings or industrial
      transition, a description of Sweden's extensive labor
      policies relating to these issues is included. Paral-
      lels are drawn between the size and industrial nature of
      New England and Sweden.

170. Herron, Frank. *Labour Market in Crisis: Redundance at
      Upper Clyde Shipbuilders*. London: Macmillan Press,
      1975. 215 pp.
      Examines the behavior of redundant workers and the
      effectiveness of public manpower policies by evaluating
      workers laid off by Upper Clyde Shipbuilders Ltd. in
      1969 and 1970.

171. Hooks, Gregory. "The Policy Response to Factory
      Closings: A Comparison of the United States, Sweden,
      and France." *The Annals of the American Academy of
      Political and Social Science 475* (September 1984):
      110-24.
      Compares three policy responses to the recent reces-
      sion: conservative free-market (the response by the
      United States), liberal industrial (the French re-
      sponse), and social welfare (the Swedish response). The
      comparison indicates that a response more interven-
      tionist than relying on the market is possible and
      advisable, but the industrial or social welfare policy

alone cannot fully address the problem of plant
closings.

172. Kaldor, Donald R.   "Rural Income Policy in the United
      States." *Externalities in the Transformation of
      Agriculture: Distribution of Benefits and Costs from
      Development.* Ames, Iowa: Iowa State University Press,
      1975. pp. 143-63.
      Discusses three major areas of social concern with
      regard to the income situation in rural America: (1)
      low rates of return to labor and capital in farming, (2)
      declining economic viability of many rural towns, and
      (3) the plight of the rural poor. Kaldor discusses the
      economic decline experienced by many rural towns as a
      result of declining farm numbers and advances in auto-
      motive transportation that occurred in the 1950s and
      1960s. The author observes that there have been few
      powerful interest groups representing rural townspeople
      or the rural poor similar to those speaking for
      commercial agriculture.

173. Keyes, Robert J., Edward Tunis, J.E. Reeves, R.D.
      Hutchinson, Andre Lemieux, Nancy Porter, and Mark
      Kennedy. *Report of the Task Force on Mining
      Communities.* Ottawa, Ontario: Energy, Mines, and
      Resources Canada, 1982. 130 pp.
      Focuses on mining communities and the impacts of mine
      closure upon them. It suggests possible steps that
      could be taken to alleviate distress both in reces-
      sionary periods and in permanent closures. Shared risk
      is a basic tenet of this study. The Task Force firmly
      believes that the burden of responsibility for mining
      communities in Canada must be shared by all involved--
      industry, labor, governments, and the mining communities
      themselves.

174. Langerman, Philip D., Richard L. Byerly, and Kenneth A.
      Root. *Plant Closings and Layoffs: Problems Facing
      Urban and Rural Communities.* Des Moines, Iowa: Drake
      University, 1982. 143 pp.
      Summarizes findings of a review of displaced worker
      and community experiences following closure of two major
      industrial plants in Des Moines. Sixty-seven displaced
      workers and spouses were interviewed. The aim of the
      study was to identify the traumatic areas of concern and
      to propose strategies for other communities to follow.

175. Levan, Charles L. "Analysis and Policy Implications of
     Regional Decline." *American Economic Review* 76, no. 2
     (1986): 308-12.
     Examines recent regional shifts of employment in the
     United States and discusses implications for economic
     theory and policy.

176. Lustig, R. Jeffrey. "The Politics of Shutdown:
     Community, Property, Corporatism." *Journal of
     Economic Issues* 19, no. 1 (March 1985): 123-52.
     Examines the relationship of large-scale enterprise to
     the community. Lustig explores the struggle between an
     undemocratic corporate power over communities and the
     revived recognition of the public interest and of prop-
     erty rights resting in the community.

177. McCarthy, James E. *Trade Adjustment Assistance: A Case
     Study of the Shoe Industry in Massachusetts.* Research
     Report 58. Boston: Federal Reserve Bank of Boston,
     1975. 235 pp.
     Presents information on worker and firm recipients of
     assistance under the Trade Expansion Act of 1962. (The
     act allows assistance to workers who have suffered
     effects from increased imports.) A systematic sample
     consisting of 200 workers was chosen to study the worker
     program. Each worker was interviewed, and the shoe
     firms were visited to obtain information. The results
     showed that the adjustment assistance program was
     ineffective for a variety of reasons.

178. McKenzie, Richard B., ed. *Plant Closings: Public or
     Private Choices?* Washington D.C.: Cato Institute,
     1982. 164 pp.
     Presents a case against plant-closing legislation and
     similar restrictions on the free movement of capital.
     The authors question the need for such restrictions by
     first presenting empirical evidence concerning plant
     closings and relocations, and second by arguing that
     restrictions are generally counterproductive and lead to
     a loss in societal welfare. According to their analy-
     sis, restrictions on business mobility will increase
     production costs by reducing efficiency in the alloca-
     tion of resources. Resources will tend to be tied up in
     comparatively inefficient sectors, thus resulting in
     retardation of development across all regions.

179. McKenzie, Richard B. *Fugitive Industry: The Economics*

and Politics of Deindustrialization. Cambridge,
Mass.: Ballinger Publishing Company, 1983. 281 pp.
Challenges the assumptions, arguments, and empirical
case for plant-closing restrictions. McKenzie contends
that closing restrictions are in essence restrictions on
plant openings, that they will destroy more jobs than
they save, and that they dampen the country's economic
growth.

180.   Martin, Philip L. *Labor Displacement and Public Policy.*
       Lexington, Mass.: Lexington Books, 1983. 125 pp.
       Examines the many special protection programs for
       displaced workers. Martin focuses on the costs of
       displacement, job protection in the United States and
       Europe, and reform issues.

181.   Martinez, Doug. "Farm Policy Shifts: Trouble for Rural
       Counties?" *Farmline* 6, no. 3 (April 1985): 14-15.
       Points out the vulnerability of farm-dependent areas
       to shifts in farm policy and characterizes these areas
       and the difficulties they have in trying to diversify
       their economy.

182.   Mazza, Jacqueline, Virginia Mayer, Mary Chione, Leslie
       Cutler, Timothy Hauser, and Amy Spear. *Shutdown: A
       Guide for Communities Facing Plant Closings.*
       Washington, D.C.: Northeast-Midwest Institute, January
       1982. 65 pp.
       Designed as a practical reference guide for local
       decision makers concerned with the closing of a major
       local public or private facility. Presents a host of
       available ideas and strategies for use by communities
       involved in various stages of economic dislocation.
       Such strategies are subdivided by temporal stages:
       preliminary indications of plant closings, recovery, and
       achieving full recovery.

183.   Millen, Bruce H. "Providing Assistance to Displaced
       Workers." *Monthly Labor Review* 102, no. 5 (May 1979):
       17-22.
       Offers a brief review of both the collective bargain-
       ing and the statutory response to the threat of job
       loss. The programs described are reactive in that they
       were designed in reaction to decisions already made or
       on decisions as they were being formulated.

184.   National Alliance of Business. *Worker Adjustment to
       Plant Shutdowns and Mass Layoffs: An Analysis of*

Program Experience and Options. Washington, D.C.:
National Alliance of Business, 1983. 154 pp.
Attempts to develop a thorough understanding of worker
adjustment programs that have assisted, or might assist,
persons affected by plant closings and mass layoffs.
Major topics addressed include (1) the nature and extent
of the problem of worker dislocation, (2) current and
historical employment and adjustment programs, (3) a
case study of a Canadian program (the manpower Consul-
tative Service), and (4) a distillation of potential
programmatic options, including a brief sketch of key
elements of a program concept that might be developed in
the United States by the public and private sectors to
deal on a local basis with worker dislocation problems.

185.   National Labor Law Center. *Plant Closings and Runaway
       Industries: Strategies for Labor*. Washington, D.C.:
       National Labor Law Center, 1981. 40 pp.
       Examines the legal strategies available to trade
unionists and their lawyers who face the threat and
reality of plant shutdowns. Included is an examination
of the Labor Management Relations Act, a discussion of
the negotiation of contract language about prenotification, an overview of legal considerations outside the
National Labor Relations Act and of legislative
proposals to control plant shutdowns, and a discussion
of worker and community takeovers of plants.

186.   "Plant Shutdowns: States Take a New Tack." *Business
       Week* no. 2813 (October 24, 1983): 72+.
       Discusses efforts by Massachusetts and other states
and communities to pass plant-closure laws, including
early-warning requirements.

187.   Ray, E. Philip. "The Labor Relations Impact of Store
       Closings in the Retail Food Industry." *Labor Law
       Journal* (August 1980): 482-86.
       Examines some of the factors of job loss for 100,000
retail food workers who lost their job between 1975 and
1980 and discusses problems of labor-management relations during that time. Ray contends that labor and
management must go beyond the emotions of the bargaining
table to in-depth discussions of industry economics in
which labor and management are partners rather than
adversaries on issues vital to both; unions, in turn,
will need to accept the responsibilities that go along
with that relationship.

188.   Redburn, F. Stevens, and Terry F. Buss, eds. *Public
       Policies for Distressed Communities*. Lexington,
       Mass.: Lexington Books, 1982. 287 pp.
       Contains eighteen original articles that discuss the
       economic crises communities often face as a result of
       the restructuring of the national and world economies.
       Discussions of the wisdom of aid to distressed areas and
       communities and the most appropriate forms of such aid
       are shown to be highly polarized.

189.   Root, Kenneth A. *Perspectives for Communities and
       Organizations on Plant Closings and Job Dislocations*.
       Ames, Iowa: North Central Regional Center for Rural
       Development, Iowa State University, 1979. 32 pp.
       Provides an overview of the impacts affecting dis-
       placed workers, their families, and the communities in
       which they were employed. The aim is to identify prob-
       lems that can be anticipated from such shutdowns and to
       suggest viable solutions and alternatives.

190.   Roseman, Curtis C., Andrew J. Sofranko, and James D.
       Williams, eds. *Population Redistribution in the
       Midwest*. Ames, Iowa: North Central Regional Center
       for Rural Development, Iowa State University, 1981.
       222 pp.
       Discusses the demographic, geographic, historical, and
       policy aspects of the recent population redistribution
       patterns. Also discussed is the set of issues that have
       emerged with this redistribution--issues such as urban
       migrants to rural areas, industry's role in nonmetro-
       politan economic development and population change, and
       local politics.

191.   Schnitzer, Martin. *Regional Unemployment and the
       Relocation of Workers*. New York: Praeger Publishers,
       1970. 255 pp.
       Provides a general background on relocation programs
       in Europe and the United States before focusing on
       relocation practices of Sweden, Great Britain, the
       United States, Canada, France, West Germany, Norway,
       Denmark, Holland, and Belgium.

192.   Schriver, William R., Roger L. Bowlby, and Donald E.
       Pursell. "Evaluation of Trade Readjustment Assistance
       To Workers: A Case Study." *Social Science Quarterly*
       57, no. 3 (1976): 547-56.
       Evaluates the effectiveness of trade readjustment
       assistance (TRA) in aiding workers affected by a plant

shutdown. Workers at an electronics assembly plant in a large midsouthern city constituted the study population. The authors found that workers who were eligible for TRA benefits were unemployed for a longer period prior to accepting a new job compared to those who were not eligible. However, workers who received TRA benefits also received somewhat lower wage rates in their new positions than did those not receiving benefits.

193. Sclar, Elliott D. "Social Costs Minimization: A National Policy Approach to the Problems of Distressed Economic Regions." *Policy Studies Journal* 10, no. 2 (1981): 235-47.
    Makes the distinction between output-maximizing and cost-minimizing approaches to national economic policy. Sclar argues that, because the benefits of economic activity and its costs are frequently conferred upon distinct groups in society, it is not automatically true that output maximization is the best strategy, especially for the problems of distressed economic regions.

194. Shultz, George P., and Arnold R. Weber. *Strategies for the Displaced Worker.* New York: Harper & Row, 1966. 221 pp.
    Reports on the comprehensive effort to cope with mass layoffs within the framework of a collective bargaining relationship. In 1959 Armour and Company together with the Amalgamated Meat Cutters and the United Packinghouse Workers formed a committee to study the problems of displacement arising from the company's modernization program, to promote transfers within the company, and to provide retraining and relocation allowances.

195. Somers, Gerald G., ed. *Retraining the Unemployed.* Madison, Wisc.: University of Wisconsin Press, 1968. 351 pp.
    Is a collection of eight papers that evaluate the retraining programs for unemployed workers--programs established under governmental or union-management auspices. Programs in the following states are included: West Virginia, Connecticut, Tennessee, Michigan, Nebraska, and Illinois.

196. Taber, Thomas D., Jeffrey T. Walsh, and Robert A. Cooke. "Developing a Community-Based Program for Reducing the Social Impact of a Plant Closing." *The Journal of Applied Behavioral Science* 15, no. 2 (1979): 133-55.

Reports results of an innovative approach to coping with the impact of a shutdown. The experiment organized management, union, university, and community representatives in Great River, Michigan, into a temporary coalition. This group assumed responsibility for organizing complex and intense problems expected to result from sudden widespread unemployment. The paper also describes organization theory useful for understanding and evaluating the processes that took place.

197. Wendling, Wayne R. *The Plant Closure Policy Dilemma: Labor, Law and Bargaining.* Kalamazoo, Mich.: W.E. Upjohn Institute for Employment Research, 1984. 166 pp.

Attempts to answer the following questions. What is the potential for collective bargaining to alter the decision to close when continued operation is a reasonable alternative? Can bargaining over the effects of closure provide a reasonable opportunity for workers to mitigate some of the consequences? Have management and labor used formal contract negotiations to obtain protections and to develop solutions for workers and firms at risk of closure?

Effects on Public Services

198. Bills, Nelson L., and Paul W. Barkley. *Public Investments and Population Changes in Three Rural Washington State Towns.* Agr. Econ. Rpt. 236. Washington, D.C.: USDA, Economic Research Service, 1973. 26 pp. (Doc. A93.28: 236)

Analyzes public capital expenditures for public services in three rural towns in Washington undergoing changes in the size and socioeconomic composition of their population.

 *   Brownrigg, Mark. "Industrial Contraction and the Regional Multiplier Effect: An Application in Scotland." Cited above as item 43.

199. Cigler, Beverly A. *Setting Smalltown Research Priorities: The Service Delivery Dimension.* Staff Rpt. No. AGES 860818. Washington, D.C.: USDA, Agriculture and Rural Economics Division, Economic Research Service, April 1987. 24 pp.

Examines alternative options for local government service delivery and financing in rural areas and focuses on potential constraints to their use. Research gaps are identified, and topics suggested for future research with a focus on service delivery and financing options, policy implementation, and local capacity-building. Simulated case studies are suggested to meet priority research needs.

200. Debertin, David L., and Angelos Pagoulatos. "Impacts of Declining Enrollments on Educational Expenditures in Rural Areas." *North Central Journal of Agricultural Economics* 2, no. 1 (1980): 25-30.
    Uses an econometric model to analyze impacts of declining school enrollments on educational funding in rural areas in Indiana. Results suggest that declining enrollments have led to increased per pupil expenditures in rural school districts.

  * Doeksen, Gerald A. "The Agricultural Crisis As It Affects Rural Communities." Cited above as item 62.

201. Goldman, George, and Anthony Nakazawa. *Local Government Cutbacks in Hard Times*. WREP 96. Corvallis, Ore.: Oregon State University, Western Rural Development Center, 1987. 4 pp.
    Discusses methods that local governments often employ to cope with fiscal crisis, including common cutback actions, the problems and paradoxes of fiscal decline, and considerations of cutback management.

202. Hamilton, Joel R., and Richard Reid. "Rural Communities: Diseconomies of Small Size and Costs of Migration." *Growth and Change* 8, no. 1 (1977): 39-44.
    Presents some exploratory measures of economies of size for small communities and some evidence of the impact of migration on community costs.

  * Harris, Thomas R. "Methodologies for Modeling Impacts: Community Service Budgets and the Use of Microcomputers." Cited above as item 87.

203. Lassey, William R. "Impacts of Public Revenue Decline Upon Rural Services: Indicators from the State of Washington." *The Rural Sociologist* 3, no. 4 (1983): 251-54.
    Examines the effects of a decline in local, state, and federal revenues on expenditures for a range of public services in Washington counties.

204. Lawson, Michael. "The Impact of the Farm Recession on
      Local Governments." *Intergovernmental Perspective* 12,
      no. 3 (1986): 17-23.
      Uses information from ten farming-dependent states in
      the North Central, Plains, and South regions to assess
      the effect of unfavorable economic conditions in agri-
      culture on the fiscal health of local governments. The
      author concludes that property tax revenues respond
      slowly to changing economic conditions but that reduc-
      tions in state aid may pose major problems for some
      local services.

  *   Stone, Kenneth E. "Impact of the Farm Financial Crisis
      on the Retail and Service Sectors of Rural
      Communities." Cited above as item 144.

205. Voth, Donald E., and Diana M. Danforth. "Effect of
      Schools Upon Small Community Growth and Decline." *The
      Rural Sociologist* 1, no. 6 (1981): 364-69.
      Attempts to determine whether change in the presence
      or absence of rural schools and in the number of schools
      operating in a local community could be demonstrated to
      influence community growth.

Social and Psychological Effects

206. Anderson, Robert N., and Rebecca Y. Pestano. *Some
      Observations on the Socioeconomic Impacts of
      Industrial Withdrawal from a Rural Community.*
      Corvallis, Ore.: Oregon State University, Western
      Rural Development Center, November 1974. 18 pp.
      Examines workers' reactions to the planned phaseout of
      two pineapple plantations in Hawaii. The threats of
      unemployment and the disintegration of the communities
      caused the workers to assume defensive stances. Few
      anticipated leaving the plantation and effectively
      achieving competence in dissimilar employment. The
      attenuating nature of the phaseout is perceived to
      weaken family solidarity and strength.

  *   Aronson, Robert L., and Robert B. McKersie. *Economic
      Consequences of Plant Shutdowns in New York State.*
      Cited above as item 26.

207. Briar, Katharine H. *The Effect of Long-Term Unemployment on Workers and Their Families.* San Francisco: R & E Research Associates, 1978. 128 pp.
Explores the social and psychological consequences of fifty-two unemployed workers during the 1970-1972 recession in Seattle, Washington. The work is concerned with what happens to people when they are unemployed--how they feel, what they do, and how they explain to others and themselves what has happened.

208. Bubolz, Margaret J. "Family Adjustment Under Community Decline." *Communities Left Behind: Alternatives for Development* (item 224), pp. 54-66.
Draws upon previous research related to families and family responses to crises and social change to suggest a model for analyzing family response to community decline. The author indicates areas where change and adaptation in families in declining communities might be anticipated.

209. Cobb, Sidney, and Stanislav V. Kasl. *Termination: The Consequences of Job Loss.* Cincinnati, Ohio: U.S. Department of Health, Education, and Welfare, Public Health Service, 1977. 188 pp.
Reports on a longitudinal study of men whose jobs were terminated. The one hundred men and seventy-four controls were followed from before the two plants closed until twenty-four months afterwards. The focus was on physical and mental health. In the mental health sphere changes were noted in a sense of deprivation, affective states, and self identity. In the physical health area, complaints were most prominent during the period of anticipation. Physiological changes suggesting an increased likelihood of coronary disease took place, and there was an increase in arthritis and hypertension.

210. Cohn, Richard M. "The Effect of Employment Status Change on Self-Attitudes." *Social Psychology* 41, no. 2 (1978): 81-93.
Presents a theoretical model of the effect of status change on self-attitudes. This dissatisfaction is accentuated by (1) concomitant change in family income, (2) the unavailability of alternative roles and prior achievements, and (3) the lack of an external locus of cause to which to attribute job loss.

   * Dean, Lois. "Minersville: A Study in Socioeconomic Stagnation." Cited above as item 59.

211. Eisenberg, Philip, and Paul F. Lazarsfeld. "The Psycho-
      logical Effects of Unemployment." *Psychological
      Bulletin* (June 1938): 358-90.
      Explores the effects of unemployment on personality,
      the sociopolitical attitudes affected by unemployment,
      differing attitudes produced by unemployment and related
      factors, and the effects of unemployment on children and
      youth.

212. Ferman, Louis A., and Jeanne P. Gordus, eds. *Mental
      Health and the Economy.* Kalamazoo, Mich.: W.E. Upjohn
      Institute for Employment Research, 1979. 423 pp.
      Collects papers presented at a conference on mental
      health and the economy. Topics include role adaptation,
      work-related stress, the psychophysiology of stress,
      plant closing and job loss, social impacts of stress,
      unemployment, and federal legislation.
      Contains item 216.

213. Foltman, Felician F. *White- and Blue-Collars in a Mill
      Shutdown: A Case Study of Relative Redundancy.*
      Ithaca, New York: Cornell University, 1968. 130 pp.
      Attempts to understand the human stresses caused by
      permanent layoff, why and how white- and blue-collar
      workers differ in their adjustment to shutdown, and job-
      seeking and adjustment behavior. Foltman concludes that
      older workers find new employment less readily than
      younger workers, that more highly educated or skilled
      workers have a greater chance of re-employment, that
      organized community efforts to find jobs for displaced
      workers are generally unsuccessful, that displaced
      workers perceive their new job as less desirable than
      their previous employment, that blue-collar workers are
      more strongly attached to their community and less
      willing to move away, and that retraining or continuing
      education is not considered to be a realistic
      alternative by displaced workers.

214. Grayson, J. Paul. "Plant Closures and Political
      Despair." *Canadian Review of Sociology and Anthro-
      pology* 23, no. 3 (1986): 331-49.
      Deals with the workers displaced by two Toronto plant
      closures--at SKF Canada Ltd. and Canadian General
      Electric. The closures were viewed as traumatic life
      change events by former employees and their spouses, and
      the level of psychological well-being of these individ-
      uals was lower than that of the general population. The
      victims of the shutdowns viewed the closures as having a

political-economic referent, and, as a result of the
closures, they had less faith in their ability to affect
the political process than the general population. However, these persons were no more likely than the general
population to opt for radical means of change.

215. Hagen, Duane Q. "The Relationship Between Job Loss and
     Physical and Mental Illness." *Hospital and Community
     Psychiatry* 34, no. 5 (1983): 438-41.
     Reviews literature on the impact of unemployment and
     job loss on employees and their family. Hagen concludes
     that the evidence shows that job loss causes measurable
     psychological and physiological changes, contributes to
     higher levels of ill health, and is related to severe
     mental disorders as measured by suicide rates and first
     admissions to mental hospitals.

216. Kasl, Stanislav V., and Sidney Cobb. "Some Mental
     Health Consequences of Plant Closing and Job Loss."
     Mental Health and the Economy (item 212), pp. 255-99.
     Presents results of a longitudinal study of the health
     and behavioral effects of job loss and ensuing
     unemployment and/or job change experience. Male blue-
     collar workers at two plants were identified prior to
     shutdown; workers were between the age of 35 and 60,
     were married, and had worked at the plant at least three
     years.

   * Kinicki, Angelo J. "Personal Consequences of Plant
     Closings: A Model and Preliminary Test." Cited above
     as item 101.

217. Kraybill, David S., Thomas G. Johnson, and Brady J.
     Deaton. *Income Uncertainty and the Quality of Life: A
     Socio-Economic Study of Virginia's Coal Counties.*
     Bull. 87-4. Blacksburg, Va.: Virginia Agricultural
     Experiment Station, 1987. 87 pp.
     Describes and analyzes historical trends in the
     quality of life in the coal-producing counties of
     southwest Virginia. Social and economic conditions in
     the seven coal counties were compared with average
     conditions for the state of Virginia. The principal
     conclusion is that the unique economic structure of the
     coal-mining region creates a system of opportunities,
     constraints, and incentives that leads to a quality of
     life that is below the state average in most respects.
     The pattern of income resulting from the economic

structure of the region explains much of the deficiency
in quality of life.

* Leistritz, F. Larry, and Brenda L. Ekstrom.
  *Interdependencies of Agriculture and Rural
  Communities: An Annotated Bibliography.* Cited above
  as item 105.

218. Muhamad, Jusoh Nordin B. "Rural Community Influentials:
     Participation in Local Voluntary Organizations."
     Ph.D. Dissertation. Baton Rouge, La.: Louisiana State
     University, 1982. 184 pp.
     Identifies the types of variables that are possible
     predictors of organizational participation. Twelve
     counties in six southern states were sampled. The study
     suggests that ecological and situational variables are
     more important predictors of participation than indi-
     vidualistic variables.

  * Murdock, Steve H., Lloyd Potter, Rita R. Hamm, Kenneth
    Backman, and Don E. Albrecht. "The Implications of
    the Current Farm Crisis for Rural America." Cited
    above as item 120.

219. Pearlin, Leonard I., Morton A. Lieberman, Elizabeth G.
     Menaghan, and Joseph T. Mullan. "The Stress Process."
     Journal of Health and Social Behavior 22 (December
     1981): 33/-56.
     Uses longitudinal data to observe how involuntary job
     disruption, chronic life strains, self concepts, coping,
     and social supports come together to form a process of
     stress, as indicated by depression.

220. Porter, Robert A., John A. Peters, and Hilda R. Heady.
     "Using Community Development for Prevention in
     Appalachia." *Social Work* 27 (July 1982): 302-7.
     Presents community development as a strategy for
     achieving goals of prevention of physical and mental
     illness in small communities in Appalachia. The authors
     emphasize the organization of social structures and
     collective efforts in problem solving as a way of re-
     ducing stress, altering lifestyles, and enhancing levels
     of physical and mental health in these vulnerable
     communities.

  * Root, Kenneth. *Companies, Mines and Factories--
    Shutdowns, Closures and Moves: A Bibliography.* Cited
    above as item 128.

221. Raup, Philip M. "The Impact of Trends in the Farm Firm
     on Community and Human Welfare." *Emerging and
     Projected Trends Likely to Influence the Structure of
     Midwest Agriculture, 1970-1985* (item 41), pp. 104-15.
     Examines several aspects of the effects of the chang-
     ing farm structure on rural communities by discussing
     environmental controls in production, unequal sharing in
     the increases in wealth in rural areas, and evaluating
     the benefits of urban versus rural communities.

222. Root, Kenneth. "The Human Response to Plant Closures."
     *The Annals of the American Academy of Political and
     Social Science* 475 (September 1984): 52-65.
     Compares the workers' responses to job loss after the
     1975 closure of a Mason City, Iowa, firm, the 1980
     closure of an Edgerton, Wisconsin, firm, and the 1981
     closure of a Des Moines firm. Contrary to workers in
     the 1975 closure study, the workers in the 1981 Des
     Moines study did not view their job loss as providing
     new opportunities. Responses from those involuntarily
     unemployed indicate that they were more likely to rely
     on the informal support of extended families during
     unemployment but that they were uncertain as to the
     extent of that support in the long run. Those forced
     into the formal support system found the stigma nearly
     overwhelming; a feeling of general aimlessness existed.

   * Rose, David, Carolyn Vogler, Gordon Marshall, and Howard
     Newby. "Economic Restructuring: The British Experi-
     ence." Cited above as item 130.

   * Taber, Thomas D., Jeffrey T. Walsh, and Robert A. Cooke.
     "Developing a Community-Based Program for Reducing the
     Social Impact of a Plant Closing." Cited above as
     item 196.

223. Thomas, L. Eugene, Esther McCabe, and Jane E. Berry.
     "Unemployment and Family Stress: A Reassessment."
     Family Relations 29 (1980): 517-24.
     Reports on two small-scale studies that found that
     unemployment of a group of managers and professionals
     did not place a strain on family relationships, although
     some personal distress occurred. Three causes for the
     apparent change in the impact of unemployment were
     noted: (1) improved financial support for unemployed
     workers, (2) decline in the psychological importance of
     work, and (3) changing sex roles.

* Western Analysis. *An Economic and Social Assessment of the Anaconda Company Smelter Closure: Anaconda, Montana.* Cited above as item 153.

224. Whiting, Larry R., ed. *Communities Left Behind: Alternatives for Development.* Ames, Iowa: Iowa State University Press, 1974. 151 pp.

   Identifies some of the characteristics, entities, and amenities desirable to human life within rural communities. The book covers such topics as quantitative dimensions of decline and stability, social and family adjustment to decline, service structures, enhancing economic and social opportunity, and feasible options for social action and economic development. Contains items 1, 63, 208, 225, 668.

225. Wilkinson, Kenneth P. "Consequences of Decline and Social Adjustment To It." *Communities Left Behind: Alternatives for Development* (item 224), pp. 43-53.

   Argues that community decline, like community development, is a pervasive process reflected at all levels in a local society--in the demographic and ecological responses through which a population seeks to balance its size with its sustenance organization, in the institutional patterns and organizational structures through which daily social life is lived, in the efforts of groups to alter or improve local conditions of life, and in the feelings people have about the local society. Wilkinson describes the social processes that accompany loss of population, decreased collective viability, and lessening of the collective spirit or sense of community.

Economic Revitalization

General Topics

* Adams, Bert N. "The Small Trade Center: Processes and Perceptions of Growth or Decline." *The Community: A Comparative Perspective.* Cited above as item 22.

226. Barbe, Nancy, and June Sekera. *States and Communities: The Challenge for Economic Action.* Washington D.C.: National Congress for Community Economic Development, 1983. 154 pp.
Discusses a wide variety of innovative strategies and activities that states and communities can implement together through community-based economic development organizations. State powers and resources to influence economic development are reviewed. Topics include debt financing, direct state investment, regulation of financial markets and activities, tax incentives, block grants, education and training, transfer payment reinvestment, agriculture development policy, enterprise zones, and plant closing and dislocations.

227. Baugher, Shirley, and Ayse Somersan, eds. *Proceedings of A New Agenda for Rural America Conference.* Published jointly by the Minnesota Extension Service (University of Minnesota), St. Paul, Minn., and the University of Wisconsin-Extension, Madison, Wisc., 1987. 211 pp.
Contains sixteen papers presented at a conference designed to provide a perspective on the rural crisis, to explain how the rural economy works, to suggest appropriate policies, and to develop an agenda for revitalizing rural America.

228. Bender, Lloyd D., Bernal L. Green, Thomas F. Hady, John A. Kuehn, Marlys K. Nelson, Leon B. Perkinson, and Peggy J. Ross. *The Diverse Social and Economic Structure of Nonmetropolitan America.* Rural Dev. Res. Rpt. No. 49. Washington, D.C.: USDA, Economic Research Service, 1985. 28 pp. (Doc. A93.41:49)
Identifies seven distinct types of rural counties according to their major economic base, presence of federally owned land, or population characteristics.

The types are farming dependent, manufacturing dependent, mining dependent, government functions, persistent
poverty, federal lands, and retirement settlements.
Seven U.S. maps by county are included.

229.   Borich, Timothy O., James R. Steward, and Harlowe Hatle.
        "The Impact of a Regional Mall on Rural Main Street."
        The Rural Sociologist 5, no. 1 (1985): 6-9.
        Explores the effect that the 1980 opening of a
        regional shopping mall in Sioux City, Iowa, had on the
        retail trade of communities in the adjacent four-county
        area. The mall's development was the culmination of a
        series of legal battles waged among municipal and county
        governments, real estate developers, and merchant
        associations.

230.   Bradshaw, Ted K., and Edward J. Blakely. *Rural Com-
        munities in Advanced Industrial Society: Development
        and Developers*. New York: Praeger Publishers, 1979.
        188 pp.
        Hopes to fill the gap between rural socioeconomic
        conditions described in literature and those observed in
        reality by examining rural economic developments in
        California.

231.   Brake, John R. "Capitalizing Agriculture in Coming
        Years." *Emerging and Projected Trends Likely to
        Influence the Structure of Midwest Agriculture, 1970-
        1985* (item 41), pp. 28-54.
        Presents a background for understanding credit
        institutions in light of future needs, evaluates the
        farm credit system and the Farmers Home Administration
        programs, and suggests problem-oriented research that
        could improve credit arrangements and the functions of
        credit institutions.

232.   Brinkman, George, ed. *The Development of Rural America*.
        Lawrence, Kans.: The University Press of Kansas, 1974.
        140 pp.
        Collects the presentations of six top professional
        economists in the field of rural development: the
        philosophy and process of community development (J.
        Carroll Bottum), the emergence of area development
        (Richard Hausler), demographic trends of the U.S. rural
        population (Calvin Beale), the condition and problems of
        rural America (George Brinkman), systems planning
        (Luther Tweeten), the use of natural resources (Emery N.

Castle), and rural poverty and urban growth (Niles M. Hansen).

233. Brown, David L. "Farm Structure and the Rural Com-
      munity." *Structure Issues of American Agriculture.*
      Agr. Econ. Rpt. 435. Washington, D.C.: USDA, Eco-
      nomics, Statistics, and Cooperatives Service, 1979.
      pp. 283-87. (Doc. A1.107:438)
      Examines the effects of changes in transportation,
      communication, and structural changes in agriculture on
      small towns. More efficient transportation and com-
      munication have led to the specialization of small
      towns. Structural changes not only cause small towns to
      become less viable centers of farm inputs and marketing
      but also cause businesses and institutions to merge or
      consolidate.

234. Christenson, James A., and Jerry W. Robinson, Jr., eds.
      Community Development in America. Ames, Iowa: Iowa
      State University Press, 1980. 245 pp.
      Begins with a discussion of major concepts surrounding
      community development (CD), provides a history of CD in
      the United States, critiques specific approaches to CD
      (the technical assistance approach, the self-help
      approach, and the conflict approach), and closes with a
      discussion of the role of CD professionals.

235. Coppedge, Robert O. *Small Town Strategy: To Grow or Not
      to Grow: Questions about Economic Development.* WREP
      53. Corvallis, Ore.: Oregon State University, Western
      Rural Development Center, 1982. 6 pp.
      Is designed to help communities decide whether or not
      further local economic growth is possible and desirable.
      A discussion outline is included to facilitate community
      analysis of the costs and benefits of growing or not
      growing.

  * Corden, W. Max, and J. Peter Neary. "Booming Sector and
      De-Industrialisation in a Small Open Economy." Cited
      above as item 53.

236. Crecink, J.C. *Sharing in Economic Growth: The Missis-
      sippi Experience.* Agr. Econ. Res. Rpt. 136. Missis-
      sippi State: Agr. and Forestry Exp. Sta., July 1982.
      59 pp.
      States that rural counties in Mississippi are sharing
      in the economic growth of the state at least equally
      with average nonurban counties and are approaching the

growth rates of the urban counties. Per capita income
is increasing at a faster rate in rural counties whereas
the dollar gap is widening. The competitive share
claimed by the rural counties is increasing both for
employment and income. Manufacturing now employs more
people and creates more income in rural counties than
does any other work sector. Transfer payments are the
largest single income sector for all three county
groupings.

237. Davidson, B. R. "The Effect of Agriculture on Country
     Town Population in the Grazing and Wheat Growing
     Regions of New South Wales." *Review of Marketing and
     Agricultural Economics* 44, no. 4 (1976): 147-64.
     Attempts to identify the factors that determined the
     rate of growth of the populations of country towns in
     the grazing and wheat-growing regions of New South Wales
     between 1958 and 1971. The town population increased
     even though farm population declined during the period
     studied. In the Wheat and Sheep Zone and on the
     Northern Tablelands the rate of growth of country town
     population appeared to be determined by the rate of
     growth in gross revenue from agriculture. In all other
     regions agricultural factors appeared to have little
     effect on the rate of growth of country towns.

238. Davidson, Claud M. "Impact of Changing Land Use on
     Industrial and Retail Activities on the Texas High
     Plains." *Social Science Journal* 18 (January 1981):
     93-105.
     Investigates the impact of changing land use on
     industrial and retail activities in the Texas High
     Plains region from 1964 to 1979, and presents a method-
     ology applicable to other areas. Davidson examines
     changing agricultural systems, manufacturing patterns,
     and population and retail patterns.

239. Deaton, Brady. "A Development Alternative for Rural
     America." *Growth and Change* 6, no. 1 (1975): 31-37.
     Advances the argument for taking a new look at the
     importance of community development corporations as
     tools for rural development planning and mechanisms to
     alleviate serious problems of alienation and economic
     impoverishment.

240. Denman, Anne Smith, ed. "Design Resource Book for Small
     Communities." *Small Town* 12 (November-December 1981):
     1-96.

Focuses on case studies in successful public design
projects in small towns across the United States.
Ingenuity in funding, planning, and getting technical
assistance in design is highlighted.

241. Dillman, Don A., and Daryl J. Hobbs, eds. *Rural Society
in the U.S.: Issues for the 1980s.* Boulder, Colo.:
Westview Press, 1982. 437 pp.
Contains forty-one articles that define and clarify
problems facing rural America in the 1980s. Topics
include the reversal of nonmetropolitan migration loss,
energy, technology, rural-urban differences, rural
families, youth, elderly, minorities, women, poverty,
public services, transportation, employment, education,
housing, recreation, community development, needs
assessment surveys, indicators of well-being, impact
assessment, the structure of agriculture, part-time
farming, and natural resources.

242. Edwards, Clark. "Spatial Aspects of Rural Development."
Agricultural Economics Research 33, no. 2 (1981): 11-
24.
Reviews literature that focuses on the functional
relationships between geographic space and rural
development. Spatial considerations affect the size and
location of individual firms, and they affect geographic
patterns of economic activity and the formation of
regions. Three empirical approaches to regionalization
are reviewed--administrative, homogeneous, and functional. Rurality is defined according to the concepts of
central place, hinterland, and hierarchy.

243. Edwards, Clark. "The Bases for Regional Growth." *A
Survey of Agricultural Economics Literature.* Vol. 3,
*Economics of Welfare, Rural Development, and Natural
Resources in Agriculture, 1940s to 1970s.* Edited by
Lee R. Martin. Minneapolis: University of Minnesota
Press, 1981. pp. 159-282.
Reviews the literature in the area of regional growth
and describes five principles or theories that have been
variously considered in the literature of economics as
bases for growth. An extensive list of references is
included.

244. Erdmann, Robin J., Harlan Gradin, and Robert O. Zdenek.
Community Development Corporation Profile Book.
Washington, D.C.: National Congress for Community
Economic Development, 1985. 110 pp.

Provides in-depth information on the accomplishments
of eighteen community-based economic development
organizations operating in diverse geographic, ethnic,
political, social, and economic environments. Each
organization is profiled, and a summary of its accomplishments is given for such areas as job creation,
business development, housing, and service delivery.
The rural locations are in Alaska, Maine, Louisiana,
Mississippi, Arizona, New Mexico, Wisconsin, Kentucky,
Vermont, and New Hampshire.

245. Faas, Ronald C., Gary W. Smith, and Ronald L. Tackett.
      The Employment Structure of Washington Counties: 1980.
      WRDC 34. Corvallis, Ore.: Oregon State University,
      Western Rural Development Center, 1986. 23 pp. plus
      appendix.
      Presents estimates of the 1980 employment structure
      of Washington's thirty-nine counties. Basic concepts of
      economic structure are outlined, and measures of county
      employment structure are defined. The measures provide
      indications of (1) economic dependency (amount and
      percent of total "basic" employment in each sector); (2)
      economic specialization (location quotients and net
      exports), and (3) import substitution potential (net
      imports).

246. Fear, Frank A., and Harry K. Schwarzweller, eds.
      *Research in Rural Sociology and Development: Focus on
      Community.* Vol. 2. Greenwich, Conn.: JAI Press,
      1985. 280 pp.
      Explores several aspects of rural community develop-
      ment: theoretical perspectives, community responses to
      growth, strategies for enhancing rural community
      development, and linking research with community action.

247. Fitzsimmons, Stephen J., and Abby J. Freedman. *Rural
      Community Development: A Program, Policy, and Research
      Model.* Cambridge, Mass.: Abt Books, 1981. 524 pp.
      Evaluates the Experimental Schools projects introduced
      in ten U.S. rural communities and analyzes various
      community effects of the projects in terms of fifteen
      community sectors, such as education, economic base,
      government operations, and social services. An analytic
      paradigm is used to trace these impacts through the
      whole system of sectors. Qualitative and quantitative
      data were collected by social scientists who lived in
      the ten communities for several years.

248. Fournier, Gary M., and David W. Rasmussen. "Real
        Economic Development in the South: The Implications of
        Regional Cost of Living Differences." *The Review of
        Regional Studies* 16, no. 1 (1986): 6-13.
        Presents estimates of the cost of living for the
      forty-eight contiguous states and uses the estimates to
      adjust relative measures of economic development for
      individual states and the four major regions of the
      United States. The authors show the impact of cost-of-
      living adjustments on the per capita income measure of
      regional economic development. Because of the relative-
      ly low cost of living in the South, the level of
      economic development is often underestimated.

249. Friedmann, John, and William Alonso, eds. *Regional
        Development and Planning: A Reader*. Cambridge, Mass.:
        M.I.T. Press, 1964. 722 pp.
        Contains thirty-five articles grouped into four major
      topics: space and planning, location and spatial
      organization, theory of regional development (resources
      and migration, the role of the city, and problems of the
      rural periphery), and national policy for regional
      development (organization for regional planning,
      objectives and evaluation, and regional development
      strategies).

   * Fuguitt, Glenn V. "County Seat Status as a Factor in
        Small Town Growth and Decline." Cited above as item
        6.

250. Gabel, Medard, and Robert Rodale. "Regenerating the
        Economy Through Growth in Self-Reliance." *The Rural
        Sociologist* 4, no. 6 (1984): 420-23.
        Argues that regional and local economies would grow if
      more of its goods for its own needs were produced
      locally, thereby exporting fewer dollars from the area.
      The authors' approach, the Regenerative Zone Development
      Plan, calls for the economy to despecialize itself and
      produce a more diverse set of products.

251. Ghatak, Subrata, and Ken Ingersent. *Agriculture and
        Economic Development*. Baltimore, Md.: Johns Hopkins
        University Press, 1984. 380 pp.
        Analyzes agriculture's role in the development of
      Third World countries, identifies barriers to agricul-
      tural development, and examines remedial policies to
      foster more rapid development. Some specific topics
      covered include the theory of rent, efficient resource

use, technical change, supply response, food supplies,
and international trade.

252. Hamilton, J.R., D.V. Peterson, and R. Reid. *Small Towns
      in a Rural Area: A Study of the Problems of Small
      Towns in Idaho.* Res. Bull. No. 91. Moscow, Idaho:
      Agr. Exp. Sta., University of Idaho, 1976. 126 pp.
      Focuses on six rural small towns and their businesses
      to isolate and examine some of the economic forces that
      pressure community residents and merchants to ultimately
      shape and reshape their towns.

253. Harmston, Floyd K. *The Community as an Economic System.*
      Ames: Iowa State University Press, 1983. 333 pp.
      Is an introductory text in community economics.
      Chapters cover the community economic system, barter,
      the community multiplier, location theory, the economic
      effects of public action, roles of people in economic
      activity, change, community dynamics (growth, decline,
      and stagnation), and methodologies useful in community
      analysis.

254. Hauswald, Edward L. "The Economically Distressed
      Community: A Synoptic Outline of Symptoms, Causes and
      Solutions." *Journal of Community Development Society*
      2, no. 2 (1971): 96-105.
      Lists symptoms of, causes of, and broad programs for
      dealing with community development situations that
      reflect particularly localized unsatisfactory economic
      conditions. It is a checklist for lay practitioners of
      policymaking.

255. Heady, Earl O. "Rural Development and Rural Communities
      of the Future." *Rural Industrialization: Problems and
      Potentials.* Edited by Larry R. Whiting. Ames, Iowa:
      Iowa State University Press, 1974. pp. 136-50.
      Points out that the crux of the rural development
      problem is one of inequity in the distribution of gains
      and costs of technological economic development at state
      and national levels. Heady identifies the nature,
      location, and extent of inequities falling on rural
      communities and their various population strata and then
      evaluates alternative means of alleviating or redressing
      them. In favored locations, some of these inequities
      can be erased through industrialization. In a greater
      number of locations, however, inequities can be removed
      only through entirely different means and programs.

256. Heartland Center for Leadership Development. *The Entrepreneurial Community Case Study Project Identifying 20 Clues to Rural Community Survival.* P.O. Box 81806, Lincoln, Nebr. 68501, 1987. 20 pp.
Presents case studies of five rural Nebraska communities that were selected from among twenty identified as surviving the economic trends stemming from the current agricultural crisis. From these studies, a list of possible clues to rural community survival was developed.

257. Hines, Fred, Mindy Petrulis, and Stan Daberkow. "An Overview of the Nonmetro Economy and the Role of Agriculture in Nonmetro Development." *Interdependencies of Agriculture and Rural Communities in the Twenty-first Century: The North Central Region* (item 269), pp. 15-40.
Presents a historical and current overview of the economic conditions in metropolitan and nonmetropolitan America and provides insights into the role agriculture plays in nonmetropolitan development. The focus is on Midwestern states.

258. Hobbs, Daryl J. "Rural Development: Intentions and Consequences." *Rural Sociology* 45, no. 1 (1980): 7-25.
Describes a frame of reference for rural development research by emphasizing the identification and assessment of consequences for people and communities of programs and policies undertaken in the name of rural development. Hobbs emphasizes that researchers must be aware that development is political and concerned with values and that many of the features of prevailing developmental ideology have produced nondevelopmental outcomes.

259. Hogg, David H., and Douglas Dunn. *Small Town Strategy: Marketing the Uniqueness of Small Towns.* WREP 57. Corvallis, Ore.: Oregon State University, Western Rural Development Center, 1982. 11 pp.
Relates the science of marketing to communities. A small town can strengthen its local economy as a result of business people and concerned citizens collectively identifying and capitalizing on that community's special uniqueness. Seven simple techniques are provided to help residents of a small town identify and market what is unique about their community. A case example is included.

260. Honadle, Beth Walter. *Economic Development For Rural
      Revitalization: A Handbook.* Washington, D.C.: USDA,
      Cooperative Extension Service, 1987. 35 pp.
      Examines economic development programs in view of the
      rural economic conditions of the mid 1980s. Major
      sections deal with defining the problems and analyzing
      policy options. Selected case studies of how extension
      has assisted communities in conducting economic develop-
      ment activities are presented, and a list of resources
      (e.g., federal agencies, professional associations) is
      presented.

261. Honadle, Beth Walter. "A National Overview of Exten-
      sion's Work in Downtown Revitalization." Paper
      prepared for the Downtown Revitalization and Small
      City Development Conference, April 13-15, 1987,
      University of Wisconsin, Madison. 13 pp. Available
      from the author at the USDA, Extension Service,
      Washington, D.C.
      Reviews the Cooperative Extension Service's work in
      downtown revitalization, which encompasses areas from
      architectural design and historic preservation to
      commercial sector development. The report is based on
      annual accomplishment reports provided by Cooperative
      Extension Services, a survey of Extension Community
      Resource Development programs, and case material
      provided by extension staffs.

262. Honadle, Beth Walter. *Public Administration in Rural
      Areas and Small Jurisdictions: A Guide to the Litera-
      ture.* New York: Garland Publishing, 1983. 146 pp.
      Annotates 426 works on the administration of human and
      fiscal services; on development; and on government
      management, administration, organization, and service
      delivery in small communities and rural areas.

263. Honadle, Beth Walter. "The Role of the Cooperative
      Extension Service in Economic Development." Paper
      prepared for the Conference on the Small City and
      Regional Community, March 20-21, 1986 at Stevens
      Point, Wisc. 27 pp. Available from the author at the
      USDA, Extension Service, Washington, D.C.
      Relates the historical role of the Extension Service
      in community economic development, presents examples of
      programs currently in place, and discusses future high
      priority challenges.

264. Hope, Kempe R. "Social Change and Rural Regional
      Community Development in the United States." *Com-
      munity Development Journal* 15, no. 2 (1980): 110-16.
      Examines the perspectives and dimensions of social
      change and regional community development in the rural
      United States. The conceptual argument is on the need
      and nature of social change and community development as
      an effort against rural poverty.

265. House, J.D. *The Challenge of Oil: Newfoundland's Quest
      for Controlled Development.* Social and Economic
      Studies No. 30. St. John's, Newfoundland, Canada:
      Memorial University of Newfoundland, Institute of
      Social and Economic Research, 1985. 326 pp.
      Focuses on the attempt by the Province of Newfoundland
      to manage oil development to achieve balanced and
      sustained economic growth. Newfoundland has been
      primarily dependent on a handful of resource-based
      industries characterized by limited local processing of
      their products and by external ownership and control.
      Because of a lack of growth (or even decline) in these
      industries and an inability to stimulate the development
      of other sectors, the province has experienced high
      rates of unemployment and outmigration for several
      decades.

266. Industry Task Force on Community Revitalization. *A New
      Frontier for Business Opportunities: A Handbook for
      Private Initiative in Community Revitalization.*
      Washington, D.C.: American Bankers Association, circa
      1980. 102 pp.
      Describes how to organize a volunteer task force for
      community revitalization, identify governmental issues,
      address housing needs, develop contacts with the news
      media and within the community, and seek funding
      assistance.

267. Keeble, David, Peter L. Owens, and Chris Thompson. "The
      Urban-Rural Manufacturing Shift in the European
      Community." *Urban Studies* 20 (1983): 405-18.
      Documents, for the first time at the European Com-
      munity (EC) scale, a relative shift of manufacturing
      industry from highly urbanized to rural regions during
      the 1970s. This shift is evident in terms of gross
      domestic product, industrial output, and manufacturing
      employment and has occurred despite an urban region
      structural bias towards more modern, viable industries
      such as electronics, aerospace, and vehicles. Moreover,

the shift characterizes every individual EC country for
which data are available. The degree to which the data
are consistent with three different explanatory view-
points (focusing on production cost differences, the
impact of constrained locations, and capital restructuring) is also considered.

268. Kelly, P.D., P.C. Riethmuller, and L.O. Dollisson.
     "Factors Associated with Changing Activity Levels in
     Rural Local Government Authorities in Southern
     Queensland." *Quarterly Review of Agricultural
     Economics* 31, no. 1 (1978): 151-67.
     Examines interrelationships between rural and nonrural
     sectors and determines the likely spillover effects on
     regional economic activity that economic change might
     precipitate. This exploratory study is directed towards
     the identification of characteristics associated with
     changes in four indicators of regional economic ac-
     tivity--population, value of rural production, value
     added in manufacturing, and value of retail sales.

269. Korsching, Peter F., and Judith Gildner, eds. *Inter-
     dependencies of Agriculture and Rural Communities in
     the Twenty-first Century: The North Central Region.*
     Ames, Iowa: North Central Regional Center for Rural
     Development, Iowa State University, 1986. 230 pp.
     Collects papers on the nature of changes occurring in
     agriculture and rural communities. Two major questions
     were addressed at the conference: What is the role of
     the agricultural sector in a program of rural develop-
     ment? How can rural development programs improve both
     agricultural and nonagricultural sectors of rural
     America?
     Contains items 257, 271, 669.

270. Kuehn, John A., Marlys K. Nelson, and Bob McGill.
     "Research, Extension, and Community Interaction for
     Economic Decision Making." *Journal of the Community
     Development Society* 14, no. 2 (1983): 107-13.
     Describes the model for research and extension
     interaction used by the Local Decisions project of the
     Economic Research Service (USDA) and its use in prac-
     tice. Specific roles for researchers and community
     development specialists are noted.

271. Leistritz, F. Larry, Donald E. Albrecht, Arlen G.
     Leholm, and Steve H. Murdock. "Impact of Agricultural
     Development on Socioeconomic Change in Rural Areas."

*Interdependencies of Agriculture and Rural Communities
in the Twenty-first Century: The North Central Region*
(item 269), pp. 109-37.
Reviews the trends in agriculture in the North Central
region and the outlook for development. The authors
then discuss the effects of agricultural development on
economic, demographic, and social conditions in rural
communities.

272. Long, Celeste, and Martha Frederick. *Rural Entrepreneurship Bibliography*. Washington, D.C.: USDA,
Government Printing Office, 1988 in press.
Provides a comprehensive review of existing research
on the characteristics of entrepreneurs, the contribution of entrepreneurial firms to economic growth, and
the social and economic attributes of local communities
that help foster entrepreneurial activity.

273. Long, Huey B., Robert C. Anderson, and Jon A. Blubaugh,
eds. *Approaches to Community Development*. Iowa City,
Iowa: The American College Testing Program, 1973. 86
pp.
Describes six approaches to community development:
the community approach, the information self-help
approach, the problem-solving approach, the demonstration approach, the experimental approach, and the power-
conflict approach.

274. MacManus, Susan A. "Linking State Employment and
Training and Economic Development Programs: A 20-State
Analysis." *Public Administration Review* 46, no. 6
(1986): 640-50.
Is an analysis of the degree to which states have
promoted a linkage of economic development and employment and training programs. It examines organizational
rearrangements ranging from administration of these
activities by a single agency to collaboration by
separate organizational units through such methods as
joint data bases, planning, training, and service
delivery. MacManus concludes that the human capital
dimension of economic development will not be maximized
until powerful state education and employment agencies
also become organizationally and programmatically
linked.

275. Malizia, Emil E., and Sarah Rubin. "A Grass Roots
Development Strategy with Local Development Organiza-

tions." *Rural Development Perspectives* 1 (June 1985): 7-13.
Summarizes characteristics of successful local development organizations in California, Louisiana, Maine, North Dakota, Vermont, Kentucky, and Massachusetts. The discussion centers around the need for five factors: flexibility, leadership, local support, funding, and staff.

276. Malizia, Emil E. *Local Economic Development: A Guide to Practice*. New York: Praeger Publishers, 1985. 244 pp.
Presents a broad treatment of local economic development for persons making public-private partnerships. Specific topics covered include theories and strategies of development, financing local business development, project analysis, and the economic feasibility of projects.

277. Miller, H. Max, E. Evan Brown, and Terence J. Centner. "Southern Appalachian Handicraft Industry: Implications For Regional Economic Development." *The Review of Regional Studies* 16, no. 3 (1986): 50-58.
Is based on data obtained in a survey of southern Appalachian craftspeople and provides information on occupational entry, occupational involvement, and economic impact as well as the legal ramifications of participation by members of the handicraft industry. The analysis points out that the independence of craftspeople does not isolate them from the various state and federal employment regulations. The implications for economic development are examined, and a paradigm of development involving specialized industries is presented.

278. Miller, Michael K., Donald E. Voth, and Diana Danforth Chapman. "Estimating the Effects of Community Resource Development Efforts on County Quality of Life." *Rural Sociology* 49, no. 1 (1984): 37-66.
Estimates the impacts of Community Resource Development (CRD) programs, conducted by the Cooperative Extension Service beginning in the 1950s and 1960s, upon a variety of quality-of-life indicators for all Arkansas counties that were nonmetropolitan in 1960. Results of the analysis indicate that few of the quality-of-life indicators were affected in the direction intended by the CRD programs. Where effects were present, they were

in narrowly defined social service areas, and no "social multiplier" effects were found.

279. Miller, Robert W. *Evaluation Research in Rural Development: Concepts, Methods, Issues.* Ithaca, New York: Cornell University, Northeast Regional Center For Rural Development, n.d. 186 pp.
Provides prospective rural development evaluators with a discussion of basic evaluative procedures illustrated by relevant rural development program examples. Interest in efforts to evaluate rural development programs is not new, and methods of rural development evaluation do not differ fundamentally from those applicable to other types of development programs. However, the current demand for more widespread and intensive evaluation of rural development programs has increased the importance of examining evaluation within a context of problems, emphases, and examples especially relevant to persons with rural development interests.

280. Minnesota Department of Energy and Economic Development. *Minnesota Star City Program: An Economic Development Strategy for Your Community.* 2d ed. St. Paul, n.d. 151 pp.
Is a comprehensive training manual for communities desiring to develop an economic development strategy. Topics include organization, incorporation, components of a community profile, preparation of a one-year and a five-year plan and strategy, interpreting and using labor market information, capital improvement planning, business retention programs, and industry recruitment strategies.

281. Morrison, Peter A., and Kevin F. McCarthy. "Demographical Forces Reshaping Small Communities in the 1980s." *The Southwestern Review of Management and Economics* 3 (1983): 55-70.
Discusses demographic and socioeconomic changes that are reshaping the fortunes of small communities. In conjunction with the reduction of federal intervention in local affairs, these changes are posing new issues at the local scale. Local governments now enjoy greater autonomy, but at the cost of reduced federal aid, and each community has been forced to rely far more on its resources to manage its own growth or decline. The challenge to federal rural policy is to enable states and localities to cope more effectively with the diverse

local circumstances being generated by changing demographics.

282. Moseley, Malcolm J. "The Revival of Rural Areas in
      Advanced Economies: A Review of Some Causes and
      Consequences." *Geoforum* 15, no. 3 (1984): 447-56.
      Examines the recent growth of population in rural
      areas, particularly in Great Britain. Two sets of
      explanations are examined: employment relocation and
      residential preferences unconstrained by job locations.
      The paper then explores the consequences of these trends
      in relationship to the duplication of infrastructure,
      pressure on rural land and housing, and social change.

283. National Association of Regional Councils. *State Growth
      Promotion and Growth Management Strategies: Utilizing
      Regional Councils as Key Partners.* Special Rpt. No.
      136. 1700 K Street, NW, 13th Floor, Washington, D.C.
      20006, July 1987. 10 pp.
      Makes recommendations as to what regional councils
      should do through their state associations when trying
      to establish a role for themselves in a statewide
      development strategy.

284. The National Development Council. *Neighborhood Business
      Revitalization.* Washington, D.C., circa 1979. 119
      pp.
      Examines industrial-job development, neighborhood
      commercial revitalization, the importance of the small
      business sector in the economic base, the importance of
      long-term financing, available federal resources, local
      self-sustaining economic development delivery systems,
      job development through the private sector using
      government guarantees versus public service jobs, and
      the role of the National Development Council in the
      Neighborhood Revitalization Program.

285. Nelson, James R., and Gerald A. Doeksen. "Agricultural
      Economists in Rural Development: Responsibilities,
      Opportunities, Risks, and Payoffs." *Southern Journal
      of Agricultural Economics* 16, no. 1 (1984): 41-47.
      Summarizes rural development authorization, discusses
      demographics concerning farm and nonfarm population in
      relation to rural development support, discusses a
      taxonomy for rural development research and extension
      efforts, and presents potential results of agricultural
      economists in that field.

286. Nofz, Michael P. "Rural Community Development: The Case of Indian Reservations." *The Rural Sociologist* 6, no. 2 (1986) 69-79.
Reviews some of the problems that impede community development efforts on American Indian reservations within the context of the 1975 Indian Self-Determination and Education Assistance Act. Nofz discusses prospects for reservation development, cutbacks in federal funding for Indian programs, and budget formulation for Bureau of Indian Affairs contracts.

287. North Central Regional Center for Rural Development. *Proceedings of the Community Economic Development Strategies Conference*. Ames, Iowa: Iowa State University, 1983. 186 pp.
Collects ten papers about the following topics: future economic development, sociodemographic trends, retention and expansion, trade area analysis, entrepreneurship, cash transfers, research priorities, and the role of Extension.

288. Nothdurft, William E. *Renewing America: Natural Resource Assets and State Economic Development*. Washington, D.C.: Council of State Planning Agencies, 1984. 198 pp.
Argues that the interests of both environmentalists and industrialists are served by a resource base that is managed effectively for sustained production but that the nation has failed to make investments to maintain these resources. Nothdurft discusses economic theories and realities of natural resource limits, private markets and public purposes, enhancing resources for long-term economic growth, resource-based enterprise development, and strategic planning and management.

289. Otto, Daniel M. "Economic Linkages Between Agriculture and Other Sectors Within Rural America." *American Journal of Agricultural Economics* 68, no. 5 (1986): 1175-80.
Examines the relationship between agriculture and communities by reviewing conventional literature on the subject, presenting historical secondary data, and using input-output results to illustrate the linkages in Iowa.

290. Pigg, Kenneth E. *Rural Economic Revitalization: The Cooperative Extension Challenge*. Ames, Iowa: North Central Regional Rural Development Center, 1986. 12 pp.

Outlines some economic and demographic characteristics
of the North Central region as a whole, speculates
regarding probable futures for communities in the
region, and discusses some issues and programs for which
the Cooperative Extension Service can offer leadership.

291. Pulver, Glen C. *Community Economic Development Strat-*
      egies. G3366. Madison, Wisc.: University of Wiscon-
      sin, Cooperative Extension Service, 1986. 17 pp.
      Examines structural changes in the U.S. economy,
      sources of future employment growth, variables influenc-
      ing employment and income, a framework for policy
      development, and community economic development strat-
      egies.

292. Rainey, Kenneth D. "Forces Influencing Rural Community
      Growth." *American Journal of Agricultural Economics*
      58, no. 5 (1976): 959-62.
      Focuses on three questions: What is happening
      demographically in the rural areas of the United States?
      Can the recent growth trend be expected to continue?
      What does this imply as far as public policy and
      programs are concerned?

293. Redman, Barbara J. "Rural Development: A Critique."
      American Journal of Agricultural Economics 62, no. 5
      (1980): 1031-36.
      Reviews academic literature on past rural development
      programs and appraises the system's overall worth and
      effectiveness. Redman seeks answers to what has gone
      wrong, what has the past trend implied for human
      satisfaction, and is correction of past errors worth the
      effort?

294. Rogers, David L., Larry Whiting, and Judy A. Anderson
      eds. *An Annotated Bibliography of Rural Development*
      Research in the North Central Region. Ames, Iowa:
      North Central Regional Center for Rural Development,
      Iowa State University, 1975. 229 pp.
      Summarizes rural development research performed
      between 1967 and 1974 in the North Central region by
      scientists affiliated with Agricultural Experiment
      Stations. Literature cited is classified into eight
      categories: (1) population composition and movement,
      (2) employment, income, and wealth, (3) economic
      services and facilities, (4) social services, (5)
      natural resources, (6) individual and family decision
      making, (7) group and community decision making, and (8)

general rural development theory. Some references to
work that is relevant to each of these areas are
included even though the research may have been per-
formed by scientists outside the experiment stations
and, in some instances, outside the twelve-state region.

295. Rouhinen, Sauli. "A New Social Movement in Search of
New Foundations for the Development of the Countryside: The Finnish Action-Oriented Village Study 76 and
1300 Village Committees." *Acta Sociologica* 24, no. 4
(1981): 265-78.
Discusses the increasing disintegration of the
traditional agricultural and village structure in
Finland owing to changes in the agricultural forces of
production and in the relationship between industry and
agriculture. The research project Village Study 76 and
the 1,300 village committees created in connection with
the project are presented and evaluated as to their
capacity to generate a new form of community in the
countryside based on the activity and knowledge of the
villagers themselves.

296. Salant, Priscilla, and Robert Munoz. *Rural Industrialization and Its Impact on the Agricultural
Community: A Review of the Literature*. ESS Staff
Report No. AGES 810316. Washington, D.C.: USDA,
Economic Development Division, Economics and Statistics Service, 1981. 14 pp.
Examines literature concerning (1) the link between
farm scale and community welfare and (2) the economic
interface between agriculture and rural industrialization.

297. Southern Rural Development Center. *National Rural
Entrepreneurship Symposium*. SRDC Series No. 97.
Mississippi State, Miss., 1987. 148 pp.
Presents the papers of eighteen speakers at a rural
entrepreneurship (RE) conference. Topics include
responding to RE needs; case examples in rural settings;
the relationship of RE and the community; needs of
individual entrepreneurs; and research, education, and
policy directions.

298. Stern, Robert N., K. Haydn Wood, and Tove Helland
Hammer. *Employee Ownership in Plant Shutdowns:
Prospects for Employment Stability*. Kalamazoo, Mich.:
The W.E. Upjohn Institute for Employment Research,
1979. 219 pp.

Examines one alternative to a plant shutdown:
community-employee purchase. Three major parts are
presented. Part 1 considers the nature of the plant
location problem in terms of community-industry relationships and the effects of closing. Part 2 evaluates
the strategy involved in the investment through a cost-
benefit approach. Part 3 re-examines the community-
employee firm in terms of its control and worker
participation. Case studies illustrate the ideas
presented.

299. Summers, Gene F. "Rural Community Development." *Annual*
     Review of Sociology 12 (1986): 347-71.
     Discusses rural community development in the United
     States by tracing its historical origins, reviewing its
     status within sociology, contrasting development *of* the
     community with development *in* the community, and
     reviewing three basic strategies of rural community
     development: authoritative intervention, client-
     centered intervention, and radical reform. The author
     concludes that federal intervention policies have
     created elaborate and complex interdependencies among
     state and federal governments, the private sector, and
     communities and that rural community development
     requires a sociology that maps these relationships and
     provides explanations for changes in them.

300. Summers, Gene F., Leonard E. Bloomquist, Thomas A.
     Hirschl, and Ron E. Shaffer. *Community Economic*
     Vitality: Major Trends and Selected Issues. Ames,
     Iowa: North Central Regional Center for Rural Develop-
     ment, Iowa State University, 1987.
     Was prepared for use by rural development prac-
     titioners and extension educators. Ten sections address
     major trends and selected issues associated with rural
     community economic vitality: farming, industrializa-
     tion, employment, service industries, retirees, wage
     rates, poverty, and income inequality.

301. Swanson, L.L. *What Attracts New Residents to Nonmetro*
     Areas? Washington, D.C.: USDA, Economic Research
     Service, April, 1986. 15 pp.
     Assesses migration to nonmetropolitan counties during
     1975-1980 and analyzes to what region they were most
     likely to move. Migrants from metropolitan areas, who
     have provided much of the growth in rural areas since
     the 1970s, have tended to move to nonmetropolitan

counties that ranked high in amenities. Job-related
reasons were less important to these new residents.

302. Swanson, Linda L., and Margaret A. Butler. "Human
Resource Base of Rural Economies." *Rural Economic
Development in the 1980's: Preparing for the Future*
(item 607), pp. 7-1 to 7-23.
Indicates that nonmetropolitan counties are at a
disadvantage with regard to their labor force. Due
largely to outmigration of young people, the nonmetropolitan United States has a lower proportion of
people in the prime working ages of 20-44 than do
metropolitan areas. Discouraged workers and high levels
of work-preventing disabilities have contributed to the
lower rate of nonmetropolitan labor force participation.
In addition, nonmetropolitan residents, particularly in
the South, are less educated, as indicated by higher
high school dropout rates, fewer years of schooling
among adults, and a lower proportion of college-educated
adults.

303. Tweeten, Luther, and George L. Brinkman. *Micropolitan
Development: Theory and Practice of Greater-Rural
Economic Development.* Ames, Iowa: Iowa State University Press, 1976. 456 pp.
Presents a comprehensive look at greater-rural
development and attempts to integrate literature on
micropolitan development into a meaningful whole. The
definition of micropolitan (or nonmetropolitan) development requires that cities of up to 50,000 population,
which serve as centers of trade, services, and jobs,
must be included in addition to rural towns when
examining rural development.

304. Tweeten, Luther. "Agricultural and Rural Development in
the 1980s and Beyond." *Western Journal of Agricultural Economics* 8, no. 2 (1983): 230-40.
Examines the economic forces shaping agriculture and
rural communities to ascertain some indication of the
future of these communities. Tweeten concludes that
rural communities are now highly integrated into
national and international markets and public policies
and that farmers increasingly depend on the nonfarm
sector for production inputs and off-farm jobs. Two
principal problems of the farming industry appear to be
(1) instability caused by nature, politics, and business
cycles at home and abroad, and (2) cash-flow problems
induced by inflation or high real interest rates and by

high cash costs of farm operation, ownership, and
consumption.

305.   U.S. Congress, House. *Agricultural Communities: The
       Interrelationship of Agriculture, Business, Industry,
       and Government in the Rural Economy, A Symposium.*
       Prepared by the Congressional Research Service,
       Library of Congress. Washington, D.C.: Government
       Printing Office, October 1983. 354 pp. (Doc.
       Y4.Ag8/1: Ag8/36)
       Contains symposium proceedings on the impact of
changes in agriculture, industry, and government on
rural communities as discussed by expert analysts. The
authors cover such topics as public policy, economic and
social settings of rural communities, natural resources,
farm structure, economic development, credit institutions, and local government.

306.   U.S. Department of Agriculture. *Developing Rural
       Communities*. ERS-465. Washington, D.C.: USDA,
       Economic Research Service, 1971. 14 pp.
       Examines some of the benefits of a rural industrial
location, develops a community service check list, and
identifies sources of governmental funding for development.

307.   Weber, Bruce A. "Extension's Roles in Economic Develop-
       ment." *Journal of Extension* (Spring 1987): 16-18.
       Identifies four roles extension plays in the economic
development area: providing perspective, increasing the
knowledge base, teaching management skills, and shaping
institutional structures.

308.   Weber, Bruce A. *Trickling Down: Are Rural and Rural
       Poor Family Incomes Responsive to Regional Economic
       Growth?* Madison, Wisc.: University of Wisconsin-
       Madison, Institute for Research on Poverty, 1974. 37
       pp.
       Examines the responsiveness of family income to
regional economic growth for a sample of rural and rural
poor Wisconsin families. Ordinary least squares
regression is used to estimate the relationship between
family income change and regional income and job growth.
Results indicate that poor farm families do not get a
proportional share of additional regional income growth.

309.   Whiting, Larry R., ed. *Rural Development: Research
       Priorities*. Ames, Iowa: North Central Regional Center

for Rural Development, Iowa State University Press,
1973. 113 pp.
Examines research and educational priorities of rural
development, specifically decision making at the
household, community, state, regional, and national
levels. Economic and sociological research problems are
identified, and research resources for nonmetropolitan
development are discussed.

310. Wilkinson, Kenneth P. "Rural Community Development: A
Deceptively Controversial Theme in Rural Sociology."
The Rural Sociologist 5, no. 2 (1985): 119-24.
Discusses various conceptual and policy issues
associated with rural community development.

311. Williams, Daniel G. "Goal Conflicts in Rural Economic
Development." *Agricultural Economics Research* 32, no.
3 (1980): 21-25.
Examines two pairs of area economic objectives: gross
regional product versus local employment, and local wage
bill versus local employment. The tradeoff curve range
is greater between the first pair of objectives (a
capital-oriented and a labor-oriented objective).
Williams states that as regions become more open,
tradeoff schedules shift outward, and range and curva-
ture increase, thus intensifying the need for compromise.

Improving the Efficiency
of Existing Resources

312. Brown, Anthony. "Technical Assistance to Rural Communities: Stopgap or Capacity Building." *Public
Administration Review* 40 (1980): 18-23.
Examines the nature and effectiveness of present
technical assistance delivery as a response to the needs
of small communities and the public administrators
working in them and suggests an alternative approach
based on capacity building.

313. Center for Agricultural and Economic Development.
*Research and Education for Regional and Area Develop-
ment.* Ames, Iowa: Iowa State University, 1966. 287
pp.
Examines major problem areas in regional growth,
illustrates some technical considerations in formulating

appropriate research strategies, and presents a series
of research proposals. Twenty-five authors discuss such
topics as local services, adapting social institutions,
implementing planning goals, legal structures, managing
water resources, measuring regional development, public
policy, and simulation models.

314. Coppedge, Robert O. *Developing Local Businesses as Job
      Providers*. WREP 89. Corvallis, Ore.: Oregon State
      University, Western Rural Development Center, 1985.
      Discusses reasons why local development efforts should
begin with existing firms and outlines some steps a
community can take to improve local business conditions.

315. Crawford, Sam, Rudy Schnabel, Bruce John, and Jim
      Nelson. *Creating Jobs Through Retention, Expansion,
      and Creation of Local Firms*. Lexington, Ky.: Univer-
      sity of Kentucky Cooperative Extension Service, 1981.
      33 pp.
      Designed to assist rural areas in creating a broadly
focused economic development program designed to achieve
diversity from within a community, its existing businesses, and its people. Topics include focusing on
local firms and potential entrepreneurs, allocating
local resources to help nonmanufacturing firms, and
training in retention, expansion, and new-enterprise
development strategies.

316. DeLellis, Anthony J. *Rural Success: Case Studies of
      Successful Employment and Training Programs in the
      United States*. Richmond, Va.: Center for Public
      Affairs, Virginia Commonwealth University, 1983. 140
      pp.
      Describes fifteen successful rural employment and
training programs located in ten states. Each program
combines job training with at least one of the following: successful placement, job creation, job upgrading,
or service to populations that are traditionally
difficult to serve.

317. Doeksen, Gerald A., and Janet Peterson. *Critical Issues
      in the Delivery of Local Government Services in Rural
      America*. Staff Report AGES 860917. Washington, D.C.:
      USDA, Economic Research Service, 1987. 24 pp.
      Summarizes economic theory of community services,
reviews literature, and identifies research issues.
Current research efforts on budgets for community
services and facilities and on the production, or

delivery, function are identified as high-priority
issues. Also, the crucial topic of extending research
findings to the final user is discussed.

318. Eastman, Clyde, Robert Coppedge, and John Romanek.
     Development Strategy for Nonmetropolitan New Mexico--
     The Community Services Approach. Res. Rpt. No. 358.
     Las Cruces, N. Mex.: New Mexico State University, Agr.
     Exp. Sta., 1978.
     Is based on the concept that improved community
     services will increase a town's attractiveness to new
     industry. This study examines the range of medical and
     recreational services in New Mexico's towns and cities
     and identifies socioeconomic characteristics of towns
     that are associated with the presence of a given
     service.

319. Goffman, Irving J., J. Ronnie Davis, and John F. Morrall
     III. *The Concept of Education as an Investment.* A
     report submitted to the President's Commission on
     School Finance. Washington, D.C.: Government Printing
     Office, 1972. 117 pp.
     Discusses the role of education as a human investment
     that partially explains the rapid growth of presently
     industrialized countries. The authors make comparisons
     between human investment and physical capital investment
     and discuss the costs and benefits of education.

320. Goodwin, H.L., Jr., and Gerald A. Doeksen. "Consolida-
     tion: A Viable Option for Improving Operational and
     Financial Stability of Rural Water Systems." *Journal*
     of the Community Development Society 15, no. 2 (1984):
     59-71.
     Develops guidelines to evaluate the potential effects
     of consolidation of rural water districts. Results of a
     case study analysis of seven consolidated rural water
     districts are presented and discussed. From this, a
     generalized method that allows local decision makers to
     examine effects of consolidation is outlined. The
     method is then demonstrated by evaluating a potential
     consolidation project involving three rural water
     districts.

321. Goodwin, H.L., Jr., and Gerald A. Doeksen. *Economics of*
     Water Delivery Systems in Rural Oklahoma. Bull. B-
     745. Stillwater, Okla.: Agr. Exp. Sta., Oklahoma
     State University, 1979. 34 pp.

Examines the following topics for rural Oklahoma:
determining water needs; formulating capital cost
budgets, operating cost budgets, and appropriate rate
structures; designing a sample system; and federal and
state regulations.

322. Hansen, W. Lee. "Total and Private Rates of Return to
     Investment in Schooling." *Journal of Political
     Economy* 71, no. 2 (April 1963): 128-40.
     Develops a comprehensive set of internal rates of
     return useful in analyzing the costs and benefits of
     education. Hansen measures monetary rates of return and
     does not discuss other benefits associated with school-
     ing.

323. Harris, Thomas R., and Michael B. Mooney. *Retention,
     Expansion and Creation of Local Firms for Economic
     Development in Nevada.* BE-86-1. Reno, Nev.: Univer-
     sity of Nevada, Cooperative Extension Service, March
     1986. 8 pp.
     Discusses how to organize a retention, expansion, and
     creation team; develop an action plan; work with smaller
     or new firms; and work with retail and service firms.

324. Killian, Molly Sizer, and Thomas F. Hady. "The Economic
     Performance of Rural Labor Markets." *Rural Economic
     Development in the 1980's: Preparing For the Future*
     (item 607), pp.8-1 to 8-23.
     Reports that the economies of industrially diversified
     rural labor market areas performed better in 1969-1984
     than those with specialized economies. Of the in-
     dustrially specialized areas, only the public education/
     administration specialty areas did as well as the
     diversified economies. Areas specializing in durable
     manufacturing did the worst, on average. The other
     groups (agriculture, mining, wood products, and tex-
     tiles/apparel) varied in different aspects of perfor-
     mance, but it was hard to find much difference among
     them overall. Areas with higher proportions of high
     school graduates in the population had higher employment
     growth but not income growth.

325. Klindt, Thomas, and Curtis Braschler. *Costs, Revenues
     and Simulated Consolidation of Selected Missouri
     Counties.* Res. Bull. 949. Columbia: University of
     Missouri-Columbia, March 1969. 46 pp.
     Determines the relevant variables that affect the
     costs and revenues of county government in a specific
     area under specific conditions; develops procedures for

determining probable effects of consolidation on the
cost and revenues of specific counties; and provides a
framework that may be used by public officials in
determining the variables needed for decisions concerning county governments. Four rural counties in south-
eastern Missouri were included in the study.

326. Kuehn, John A., and Jerry G. West. *Highway Impacts on
Incomes and Employment In the Ozarks: A Study of
Statistical Relationships*. Washington, D.C.: USDA,
Economic Research Service, 1971. 26 pp.
Analyzes highway impacts on incomes and employment in
the Ozarks during the 1950s by means of rank correlation
and stepwise regression. Results indicate that highways
were not among the most critical factors in the Ozarks'
development. If new highways were built, two-lane,
paved, state-numbered roads connecting existing federal
routes and also local, paved county roads connecting
rural areas with urban centers would be more beneficial
for economic development than other highway types.
Highways with dissimilar qualities are classified into
five distinct types using the number of lanes, type of
surface, and network integration as criteria. Relevant
regional economic growth theories are also reviewed.

327. Luke, Jeff S. "New Role for Small Cities in Economic
Development." *Municipal Management* (Winter 1984): 56-
61.
Addresses the shifting roles of local government in
influencing the local economy by emphasizing that local
economic growth is becoming increasingly dependent on
the development of small business and on international
markets. Luke points out that small business development strategies should focus on such aspects as improving the quality of life through improved services to
targeted areas, providing reductions in utility fees,
employing a small business complaint person, and
providing incubators.

328. Morse, George W., John D. Rohrer, and Sam J. Crawford.
*Retention and Expansion Business Visits: A Guide for
an Effective Economic Development Program*. Bull. 728.
Columbus, Ohio: Cooperative Extension Service, Ohio
State University, 1985. 52 pp.
Aids local leaders interested in developing a business
visitation component of a retention and expansion
strategy. Information includes setting goals, organizing the visitation program, establishing early warning

systems for plant closures or reductions, sample
questionnaires, news releases, and preparing follow-up
visits.

329. Morse, George W., Roland Patzer, Ellen Hagey, Mary Lee
     Gecowets, Jack T. Sommers, and Paul R. Clapsaddle.
     *Champaign County Business Retention and Expansion
     Program, 1986 Report.* Columbus, Ohio: Ohio Coopera-
     tive Extension Service, Ohio State University, October
     1986. 60 pp.
     Presents results of the Business Retention and
     Expansion Program that used shift-share analysis,
     government data, and a survey of businesses to provide
     an advisory committee with information on which to make
     recommendations for future business retention and
     expansion programs in Champaign County, Ohio.

330. Myers, Bill, Gary Peterson, and Ted Bradshaw. "Com-
     munity Colleges Are Job Creation Vehicles in Small
     Towns." *Small Town* 17, no. 6 (May-June 1987): 26-28.
     Describes the Small Business Development Center
     Network in community colleges in Oregon. The program
     has assisted many small businesses to become viable in
     depressed rural areas of Oregon. The authors point out
     that community colleges can be partners in the overall
     economic development of their service areas.

331. National Association of Regional Councils. *Fire Defense
     Programs: Strategies for Regional Council Involvement.*
     Special Rpt. No. 128. 1700 K Street, N.W., 13th
     Floor, Washington, D.C. 20006, February 1987. 5 pp.
     Describes council involvement in starting up and
     improving fire departments and outlines the range of
     public and private grant and loan programs available to
     assist councils in equipping, organizing, and training
     fire departments.

332. National Association of Regional Councils. *Information
     Resources for Small and Rural Community Wastewater
     Treatment: Alternative Technologies for New Systems,
     Upgrading Existing Systems, Improved Management, and
     Financing.* Special Rpt. No. 134. 1700 K Street,
     N.W., 13th Floor, Washington, D.C. 20006, February
     1987. 8 pp.
     Outlines resources available in the form of literature
     and technical assistance for developing, financing, and
     maintaining adequate wastewater treatment systems in
     small and rural communities.

333. National Association of Regional Councils. *Innovative Activities of Small and Rural Regional Councils.* 1700 K Street, N.W., 13th Floor, Washington, D.C. 20006, February 1987. 18 pp.
Provides brief summaries of innovative activities in rural councils that might be duplicated elsewhere. Projects are reported by subject, such as economic development, water management, elderly services, and energy management. A contact person and phone number are provided.

334. National Main Street Center. *Small Business Retention, Expansion, and Recruitment Project.* 1785 Massachusetts Ave., N.W.; Washington, D.C. 20036.
Discusses various aspects of the above-mentioned project.

335. Nelson, J.R., B. Johnson, D.A. Wearmouth, and D.L. Folger. *An Analysis of the Economics of a Rental Apartment Project in Garfield County.* AE-8234. Stillwater, Okla.: Oklahoma State University, Dept. Agr. Econ., March 1982. 9 pp.
Presents the estimated costs and revenues for a rental apartment development. These estimates are based on research conducted at Oklahoma State University to aid in determining the feasibility of a local rental apartment project.

336. Nelson, Marlys K., and Gerald A. Doeksen. *Fire Protection Services Feasibility Guide for Local Decision-makers in the Rural Ozarks.* Bull. B-764. Stillwater, Okla.: Agr. Exp. Sta., Oklahoma State University, 1982. 56 pp.
Uses a budget analysis to evaluate the need for and the estimated annual expenses of a fire protection service. Fire apparatus and other equipment that might be best suited for small rural communities are discussed. Capital and operating expenses are projected for a hypothetical community and service area.

337. Ryan, Vernon D. "The Significance of Community Development to Rural Economic Development Initiatives." *Rural Economic Development in the 1980's: Preparing for the Future* (item 607), pp. 16-1 to 16-15.
Explains that community development takes place when local residents work together to improve the economic situation of the entire community. Community development efforts are especially important to the revitaliza-

tion of rural America's economy. One of the most
tangible benefits of such efforts is that they can
contribute to the success of local economic development
initiatives. This chapter discusses the application of
community development principles to economic development
activities.

338. Schaffer, Ron E., and Luther G. Tweeten. *Economic
      Changes from Industrial Development in Eastern
      Oklahoma.* Bull. B-715. Stillwater, Okla.: Oklahoma
      State University, July 1974. 35 pp.
      Estimates the net economic benefit of industrial
      expansion in a rural community in eastern Oklahoma.
      Economic changes in the community are examined under
      various assumptions about the refilling of previous jobs
      and the occurrence of local secondary effects. The
      spillover of economic impacts into the surrounding
      county is also examined.

339. Schultz, Theodore W. *Investment in Human Capital: The
      Role of Education and of Research.* New York: The Free
      Press, 1971. 272 pp.
      Discusses human capital in terms of investing in
      education and research. Thirteen chapters cover such
      topics as technical change, human capital analysis, the
      cost of formation by education, the rate of return in
      allocating resources to education, and institutions and
      the rising economic value of man.

340. Shallah, Salim, and Luther Tweeten. *Economic Returns to
      Technical Education at Oklahoma State Tech.* Bull. No.
      B-685. Stillwater, Okla.: Oklahoma State University,
      1970. 35 pp.
      Determines the costs and benefits incurred by in-
      dividuals and society from investment in two years of
      technical schooling and computes internal rates of
      return resulting from investment in the different fields
      of study offered at Oklahoma State Tech.

341. Sjo, John, James Trapp, and Robert Munson. *State Costs
      and Benefits from Education.* Bull. 561. Manhattan,
      Kans.: Kansas State University, 1972. 30 pp.
      Estimates the rates of return accruing to the Kansas
      economy from investment in elementary, secondary, and
      university schooling, determines average lifetime
      incomes from successively higher levels of education,
      and calculates economic loss to Kansas from net out-
      migration of persons educated at state expense.

342. U.S. Department of the Interior. *Economics of Revital-
     ization: A Decisionmaking Guide for Local Officials.*
     Prepared by the Real Estate Research Corporation. No
     city: U.S. Department of the Interior, Heritage
     Conservation and Recreation Service, January 1981. 94
     pp. (Doc. I70.8: Ec7)
     Provides a methodology for assessing the rehabilita-
     tion potential of existing buildings and for estimating
     the public costs, relative to value received, of several
     development options. The premise of the manual is that
     existing structures represent a potential development
     resource that should be thoroughly explored when
     developing revitalization plans.

*   Voth, Donald E., and Diana M. Danforth. "Effect of
     Schools Upon Small Community Growth and Decline."
     Cited above as item 205.

*   Weeks, Edward C. *Plant Modernization and Community
     Economic Stability: Managing the Transition.* Cited
     above as item 152.

*   Whiting, Larry R., ed. *Communities Left Behind:
     Alternatives for Development.* Cited above as item
     224.

Expanding and Diversifying
the Economic Base

343. Acquah, E.T., and L.J. Hushak. "Human Capital and Labor
     Turnover in Manufacturing Industries: The Case of a
     Relatively Undeveloped Region in Southeast Ohio."
     Southern Journal of Agricultural Economics 10, no. 2
     (1978): 171-76.
     Examines the role of manufacturing in the human
     capital formation and economic development of a rural
     area. A model developed by Parsons is used to test the
     statistical hypothesis that the layoff rate is related
     negatively to a firm's investment in specific human
     capital, whereas the quit rate is related negatively to
     workers' investment in specific human capital.

344. Ady, Robert M. "Criteria Used for Facility Location
     Selection." *Financing Economic Development in the
     1980s: Issues and Trends* (item 503), pp. 72-84.

Examines how facility type affects the criteria used
for the selection of a location. The results are based
upon hundreds of facility location projects that the
Fantus Company has undertaken for corporations seeking
new locations for manufacturing facilities, office
operations, R&D centers, and new and emerging enterprises.

345. Albrecht, Don E. "Agricultural Dependence and the
      Population Turnaround: Evidence From the Great
      Plains." *Journal of the Community Development Society*
      17, no. 1 (1986): 1-15.
      Points out that, although throughout our nation's
history there has been a net migration of people from
nonmetropolitan to metropolitan counties, this long
established migration trend has recently been reversed.
Data for the period 1940 to 1980 from 294 nonmetropolitan Great Plains counties show that reduced
agricultural dependence is a major factor influencing
this turnaround. The results indicate that counties
heavily dependent on agricultural employment were about
as likely to experience population declines during the
1970s as they were during earlier decades. There were
fewer such counties, however, and thus their overall
influence was reduced. The consequences of these
findings for rural communities in major agricultural
areas are discussed.

346. Anderson, Robert, and David L. Barkley. "Rural Manufac-
      turers' Characteristics and Probability of Plant
      Closings." *Growth and Change* 13, no. 1 (January
      1982): 2-8.
      Explores the significance and magnitudes of relation-
ships between selected characteristics of nonmetropolitan manufacturing plants and the probability of
closing. Results indicate that a rural community could
increase the stability of its manufacturing sector by
attracting nondurable goods producers.

347. Arkansas Department of Parks and Tourism. *Building a
      Festival: A Framework for Organizers*. Little Rock,
      Ark., 1985. 44 pp.
      Describes how to develop, plan, and run community
festivals, which can serve as an economic development
strategy. Such festivals can bring local people
together, increase local business receipts, promote
tourism, and provide entertainment.

348. Barkley, David L. "The Decentralization of High-
      Technology Manufacturing to Nonmetropolitan Areas."
      Growth and Change 19 (1988): in press.
      Seeks to determine if high-technology manufacturers
      have begun relocating employment to nonmetropolitan
      areas, and if so, which industries and geographical
      areas have participated in the decentralization process.
      Employment changes for the high-technology manufacturing
      sector are estimated for nonmetropolitan counties of
      different sizes, adjacency status, and census regions
      for the period 1975-1982. The specific high-technology
      industries that shifted employment to rural areas are
      identified, and characteristics of these manufacturers
      are analyzed to determine if the relocating industries
      adhered to the life-cycle hypothesis.

349. Barkley, David L., and Arnold Paulsen. *Patterns in the
      Openings and Closings of Manufacturing Plants in Rural
      Areas of Iowa.* Ames, Iowa: North Central Regional
      Center for Rural Development, Iowa State University,
      1979. 71 pp.
      Compares industrial migration and rates of openings
      and closings among groups of Iowa industries for a
      decade and by phases of the business cycle. It was
      found that (1) the rate of openings and closings of
      branch plants exceeded that of locally owned firms and
      (2) branch plants exhibited a greater propensity to open
      during prosperity and to close during a recession.

350. Batie, Sandra S. "Discussion: Location Determinants of
      Manufacturing Industry in Rural Areas." *Southern
      Journal of Agricultural Economics* 10, no. 1 (1978):
      33-37.
      Discusses the linear probability function method and
      the theoretical specification of the function used by
      Smith, Deaton, and Kelch (item 601) in analyzing
      location determinants of the manufacturing industry.

351. Bender, Lloyd D. "The Role of Services in Rural
      Development Programs." *Land Economics* 63, no. 1
      (1987): 62-71.
      Reviews the literature for economic rationales
      proposing that a new perspective of the role of services
      in regional economic development is appropriate. The
      author concludes that services should be considered in
      regional development plans, but for reasons and in ways
      that are traditional rather than new. Direct subsidies

by authorities to service activities may be an inappropriate general regional development emphasis.

352.   Bender, Lloyd D., and Larry C. Parcels. "Structural
       Differences and the Time Pattern of Basic Employment."
       Land Economics 59, no. 2 (1983): 220-34.
       Uses covariance analysis to examine whether economic
       structures differ significantly among rural counties and
       whether these differences are related to the time
       pattern of basic employment growth and decline.

353.   Berentsen, William H. "Regional Policy and Industrial
       Overspecialization in Lagging Regions." *Growth and
       Change* 9, no. 3 (July 1978): 9-13.
       Explores some of the long-term economic problems that
       confront lagging regions where regional development
       policies contribute to overspecialization in the
       industrial sector in an attempt to achieve employment
       growth and population stability at the expense of
       industrial diversification.

354.   Bieker, R.F. "The Distribution of Benefits from
       Industrialization in Rural Areas: Some Findings."
       *Journal of the Northeastern Agricultural Economics
       Council* 1, no. 2 (1982): 71-77.
       Examines the distribution of the benefits of in-
       dustrialization in Sussex County, Delaware. Specifical-
       ly, the study examines the impact of industrialization
       on a sample of 205 employees who were employed by eight
       manufacturing firms, which started operations in Sussex
       County between 1974 and 1977.

355.   Bloomquist, Leonard E. "Performance of the Rural
       Manufacturing Sector." *Rural Economic Development in
       the 1980's: Preparing for the Future* (item 607), pp.
       3-1 to 3-33.
       Observes that, while the rural manufacturing sector
       has had substantial growth in recent years, most of the
       growth has been in manufacturing industries that provide
       low-skill and low-wage jobs. This pattern varies by
       region and gender. The rural West has had the highest
       growth rate, and the quality of jobs provided compares
       favorably with that in other regions. The rural South
       has experienced substantial employment growth, even
       though the wage and skill levels of jobs provided are
       not as good, on average, as in other regions. By
       contrast, the rural Northeast and Midwest have relative-
       ly high-quality jobs, but employment growth has not kept

up with growth in the West and South. Finally, rural
(and urban) women tend to be employed in low-paying
manufacturing jobs that require lower skills.

356. Brinkman, George. "Effects of Industrializing Small
     Communities." *Journal of Community Development
     Society* 4, no. 1 (Spring 1973): 69-80.
     Examines the costs and benefits of attracting and
     developing new industry. The direct and indirect
     impacts on private jobs, income, property values, and
     government revenues and expenditures are examined.

357. Brinkman, George L. "Small Community Industrializa-
     tion." *Journal of Community Development Society* 3,
     no. 2 (1972): 89-92.
     Discusses some direct and indirect effects of new
     industries and multicounty cooperation for in-
     dustrialization.

358. Bryant, W. Keith. "Industrialization as a Poverty
     Policy: Toward a Micro Analysis. *Papers on Rural
     Poverty.*" Presented at the Annual Conference of the
     Southern Economic Association. Raleigh, N.C.:
     Agricultural Policy Institute, North Carolina State
     University, 1969. 82 pp.
     Examines industrial development schemes and proposals
     that have the reduction of poverty as the primary goal.
     Bryant analyzes growth and its distribution on a micro
     level and identifies leakages in the private and public
     sector that diminish the impact of industrialization on
     the poor.

359. Buck, M. Allison, Daryl J. Hobbs, D. Donald, and Nancy
     Munshaw. *Feasibility of High-Tech Company Incubation
     in Rural University Settings.* Final Report of the
     Small Business Innovation Research Program, Rural and
     Community Development, Phase I. Rolla, Mo.: Missouri
     IncuTech, Inc., 1984. 112 pp.
     Reports that it is feasible to start a high-technology
     incubator in a rural university setting (Rolla, Mis-
     souri) and that similar concepts in rural university
     settings may also be feasible.

360. Carlson, C.W. *Community Industrial Development: The
     Theory of Least Interest.* Madison, Wisc.: University
     of Wisconsin, Dept. Agr. Econ., Coop. Ext. Serv.,
     1981. 2 pp.

Describes the theory of least interest that maintains
that, when two people or parties have a degree of
interest in one another, the individual or party holding
the least interest will control the direction and
eventual outcome of that relationship. In community
development the industry is usually the holder of the
least interest.

361. Center for Rural Manpower and Public Affairs. *Labor
      Market Information in Rural Areas*. East Lansing,
      Mich.: Michigan State University, 1972. 239 pp.
      Assesses those who demand and supply rural labor
      market information. Those in need include public
      officials doing manpower planning and policymaking,
      employers seeking to locate in rural areas, and current
      and potential job seekers. Those supplying information
      include the Census Bureau, U.S. Department of Labor, and
      the U.S. Department of Agriculture.

362. Chittenden, W.H., A.E. Luloff, and J.P. Marcucci.
      *Industry in New Hampshire: Changes in the Manufactur-
      ing Sector, 1970-1978*. Res. Rpt. No. 93. Durham,
      N.H.: University of New Hampshire, Agr. Exp. Sta.,
      1982. 20 pp.
      Consists of two distinct parts: a brief explanation
      of location theory and the relative attractiveness of
      New Hampshire to manufacturers, and a detailed discus-
      sion of the patterns of industrialization that have
      developed within New Hampshire over the period 1970-
      1978. In addition, some possible explanations of these
      patterns are advanced.

363. Clair, Robert T. "The Labor-Intensive Nature of
      Manufacturing High-Technology Capital Goods."
      Economic Review (Federal Reserve Bank of Dallas) 7
      (1986): 11-19.
      Analyzes the production process for manufacturing
      high-technology equipment in an effort to determine
      whether the production characteristics of that industry
      are consistent with state objectives to encourage the
      expansion of labor-intensive industries. The research
      here uses the U.S. Department of Commerce definition of
      high-technology equipment, which consists of office,
      computing, and accounting equipment; communications
      equipment; and instruments. The results of the analysis
      show that an expansion in high-technology equipment
      manufacturing will create more jobs than expansion in

manufacturing of other types of producers' durable goods.

364. Clark, Thomas L. *A Guide for Targeting Industries in Your Community.* Montrose, Colo.: Region 10 Economic Development District, 1985. 96 pp.
Guides communities interested in conducting their own targeted industry program. It is designed to be used with the help of some economic development staff.

365. Collins, Lyndhurst, and David F. Walker, eds. *Locational Dynamics of Manufacturing Activity.* London: John Wiley & Sons, 1975. 402 pp.
Presents a cross section of research approaches (theoretical, methodological, and empirical) concerned with the locational dynamics of manufacturing activity on the regional, urban, and individual firm scale.

366. Combs, Robert P., Glen C. Pulver, and Ron E. Shaffer. *Financing New Small Business Enterprise in Wisconsin.* R3198. Madison, Wisc.: University of Wisconsin, College of Agricultural and Life Sciences, 1983. 24 pp.
Reviews information derived from a survey of 134 new small businesses, which were started in Wisconsin during 1976 and 1977. Owners were asked how they acquired the equity and debt capital to get started, how the sources changed during their first years of operation, and what problems, if any, they had encountered.

367. Community Information Exchange. *Small Business Incubators: A How-To Guide.* Washington, D.C.: National Urban Coalition, 1984. 31 pp.
Provides concise advice on a number of considerations essential to incubator projects: organization, market analysis, site analysis, building characteristics, support services, financing, management, assistance, marketing, leasing, and tenant selection. Four examples are discussed.

368. Coon, Randal C., F. Larry Leistritz, and Thor A. Hertsgaard. *Composition of North Dakota's Economic Base: A Regional Analysis.* Ag. Econ. Rpt. No. 209. Fargo, N. Dak.: North Dakota State University, Agr. Exp. Sta., 1986. 96 pp.
Uses input-output techniques to analyze the composition and changes of the economic base for North Dakota and its eight state regions for the period 1958 to 1984.

Included in the economic base activities are agriculture, mining, manufacturing, tourist expenditures, and
federal government outlays.

369. Coppedge, Robert O. *Small Town Strategy: Helping Small
      Towns Grow*. WREP 52. Corvallis, Ore.: Oregon State
      University, Western Rural Development Center, 1982. 7
      pp.
      Points out that changes in growth and migration
      patterns mean new opportunities for some small towns to
      expand their economic bases and to improve community
      facilities and services. To share in these oppor-
      tunities, however, a community must be prepared for
      aggressive pursuit of new businesses--retail and service
      businesses as well as manufacturing activities. This
      publication characterizes one small southwestern town
      that is typical of many others and outlines a develop-
      ment strategy designed for small towns like the one
      described.

370. Cottrell, William F. "Caliente." *Technology, Man, and
      Progress*. Edited by William F. Cottrell. Columbus,
      Ohio: Charles E. Merrill Publishing Company, 1972.
      pp. 67-86.
      Re-examines a small western desert town that lost its
      primary income producer, the railroad, in 1951. The
      chapter recounts previous predictions about the town's
      future and examines how the town has changed from an
      economy based on transportation to one based on ser-
      vices.

371. Daberkow, Stan G., Donald K. Larson, Robert Coltrane,
      and Thomas A. Carlin. *Distribution of Employment
      Growth in Nine Kentucky Counties*. Rural Dev. Res.
      Rpt. No. 41. Washington, D.C.: USDA, Economic
      Research Service, 1984. 35 pp. (Doc. A93.41:41)
      Is a case study that examines the distributional
      effects of rapid employment growth in a nonmetropolitan
      area. The location is a nine-county area of south
      central Kentucky. The study revealed that recent
      immigrants held a disproportionate share of better-
      paying executive and professional jobs and that they
      also held a disproportionate share of jobs in growing
      business establishments.

   *   Daicoff, Darwin W. "The Community Impact of Military
        Installations." *The Economic Consequences of Reduced
        Military Spending*. Cited above as item 58.

372. Deaton, Brady J., and Maurice R. Landes. "Rural
      Industrialization and the Changing Distribution of
      Family Incomes." *American Journal of Agricultural
      Economics* 60, no. 5 (1978): 950-54.
      Explores the hypothesis that the distributive conse-
      quences of rural industrialization are shaped by
      community and industry characteristics and by the
      demographic traits of employees and their family. An
      ordinary least squares regression analysis was used to
      determine the association between selected measures of
      these variables and dollar changes in total family
      income.

373. Dillman, D.A. "The Social Impacts of Information
      Technologies in Rural North America." *Rural Sociology*
      50, no. 1 (1985): 1-26.
      Analyzes social implications of the increased use of
      information technologies in rural North America with
      particular attention to their consequences for human
      interaction. First, the influence of technology on
      rural people's interaction patterns throughout this
      century is reviewed. Second, the increased importance
      of information as an input into the production of goods
      and services is described against a background of the
      uncertainties that exist concerning the transition to an
      information age. Last, five features of the emerging
      rural information structure are described.

374. Dorf, Ronald J. *An Econometric Analysis of Structural
      Differences Among Rural Communities and Their Affect
      [sic] on the Location of Manufacturing Plants.* Staff
      Paper P76-1. St. Paul, Minn.: University of Minne-
      sota, Department of Agricultural and Applied
      Economics, 1976. 35 pp.
      Evaluates whether quantitative structural difference
      can be discerned among rural communities and whether any
      of these structural differences are significantly
      associated with the location of manufacturing plants
      and/or growth in manufacturing employment.

375. Dorf, Ronald J., and M. Jarvin Emerson. "Determinants
      of Manufacturing Plant Location for Nonmetropolitan
      Communities in the West North Central Region of the
      U.S." *Journal of Regional Science* 18, no. 1 (1978):
      109-20.
      Develops a set of empirical measures for the criteria
      used by manufacturing firms when selecting among
      nonmetropolitan locations within the North Central

region. The main determinants were community size,
distance from urban areas, and labor force, all of which
are independent of public control.

376. Downtown Research and Development Center. *Great
      Downtown Events: How to Build Crowds and Boost
      Business.* New York, 1985. 88 pp.
      Compiles case studies of innovative promotional events
      designed to revitalize downtown areas.

377. Epping, G. Michael, and Herman S. Napier. "Plant
      Location: A Conflict Between Manufacturers and
      Community Interest Groups." *Arkansas Business and
      Economic Review* 17, no. 4 (1984): 1-8.
      Reports on a study of factors influencing location of
      manufacturing plants. Rankings of location factors by
      two manufacturing test groups were compared with those
      of a group of Chamber of Commerce presidents and town
      mayors. Considerable differences were found between the
      rankings of the manufacturers and those of the civic
      interest group. Implications of this conflict are
      discussed.

378. Erickson, Rodney A., Norma I. Gavin, and Sam M. Cordes.
      "Service Industries in Interregional Trade: The
      Economic Impacts of the Hospital Sector." *Growth and
      Change* 17, no. 1 (1986): 17-27.
      Examines the role of one of the largest consumer
      services sectors--the hospital industry--in inter-
      regional trade and assesses its impact on a regional
      economy. The analysis demonstrates the export share of
      revenue, the extent of local purchasing, and the income
      and employment-generating capacity of the hospital
      sector in a large metropolitan area.

379. Fox, William F., and C. Warren Neel. "Saturn: The
      Tennessee Lessons." *Forum for Applied Research and
      Public Policy* 2 (1987): 7-16.
      Examines the process leading to the choice of Spring
      Hill, Tennessee, as the site for the General Motors'
      Saturn Plant. Key factors influencing the location
      decision are assessed; the role of state and local
      governments receives special attention.

380. Francaviglia, Richard V. "Bisbee, Arizona: A Mining
      Town Survives a Decade of Closure." *Small Town*
      (January-February 1983): 4-8.

Discusses how the town of Bisbee, Arizona, survived
the closure of its copper mines. Economic diversification and the town's new counter-cultural population
helped turn Bisbee from a mining town to a tourist,
service, and retirement community.

381. Friedman, Robert, and William Schweke, eds. *Expanding
the Opportunity to Produce: Revitalizing the American
Economy Through New Enterprise Development.* Washington, D.C.: The Corporation for Enterprise Development,
1981. 549 pp.
Is divided into four major sections: (1) the role of
new enterprise development in economic revitalization;
(2) the socioeconomic context of development, the
economy of dependency (poverty, unemployment, etc.), and
community development experiences; (3) financing
development through public and private funds and
creating new financial intermediaries; and (4) labor
productivity, creating markets, developing new tech-
nologies, and managing development.

382. Fuller, Theodore E. *Trends in Manufacturing Among Small
Centers of Pennsylvania.* Bull. 788. University Park,
Pa.: Pennsylvania State University, 1971. 30 pp.
Describes and analyzes differential patterns of change
in the magnitude and composition of manufacturing among
centers of 1,000-24,999 population between 1960 and
1966.

383. Gillis, William, and Shahin Shahidsaless. "Effects of
Community Attributes on Total Employment Change in
Nonmetropolitan Counties." *North Central Journal of
Agricultural Economics* 3, no. 2 (1981): 149-56.
Reports a method that permits estimation of the
employment impact in communities with different attributes, resulting from an exogenous employment change.
The hypothesis tested is that community attributes, such
as per capita income, geographic location, population,
female labor force participation, median age, and
education, influence the level of community employment
in a given year.

384. Gillis, William R., and Ron E. Shaffer. "Community
Employment Objectives and Choice of Development
Strategy." *Journal of the Community Development
Society* 16, no. 2 (1985): 18-37.
Points out that successful economic development often
requires more than expanding the number of employment

opportunities in a community. In particular, there is
often a desire to create jobs for specific workers in
the community. An analysis of fifty-one manufacturing
and nonmanufacturing industries indicates a substantial
variation among different types of businesses with
respect to the type of workers hired. The analysis is
extended to form a typology of industries that is useful
to local development groups in formulating a strategy to
employ specific groups.

385. Gillis, William R., and Ron E. Shaffer. "Targeting
      Employment Opportunities Toward Selected Workers."
      Land Economics 61, no. 4 (1985):433-44.
      Relates the probability of hiring workers from
specific groups in the labor pool to the occupational
demands, degree of capital usage, size, and wage level
of employing industries. The study's aim is to provide
a means by which state and local development organizations can make a first cut on business and industry
prospects to pursue with further analysis and development efforts.

386. Gilmer, Robert W., and Allan G. Pulsipher. "Cyclical
      and Structural Change in Southern Manufacturing:
      Recent Evidence from the Tennessee Valley." *Growth
      and Change*, 17 (October 1986): 61-69.
      Examines the recovery of the manufacturing base in the
Tennessee Valley through early 1985 and finds it to be
strong compared to earlier expectations. Despite the
apparent resilience of manufacturing, the region does
have persistent and continuing employment problems.

387. Glasmeier, Amy K. "High-Tech Industries and the
      Regional Division of Labor." *Industrial Relations* 25,
      no. 2 (1986): 197-211.
      Presents results of a two-stage analysis of the
occupational structure and spatial location of high-
technology industries and employment. A model is
presented and tested using industry occupational
employment data.

388. Goeken, Wayne R., and Thomas L. Dobbs. *Rural Manufac-
      turing Development--What Influences It?* B 683.
      Brookings, S. Dak.: South Dakota State University,
      Agr. Exp. Sta., 1982. 31 pp.
      Explores how the extent and type of rural in-
dustrialization being experienced in South Dakota
differs among types of communities and local labor

markets and develops policy and planning recommendations
that can be used by rural industrial development
entities at the community, district, and state levels.

389. Goldstein, Harvey. "Community Impacts of New Industrial
      Development." *Carolina Planning* 11, no. 2 (Winter
      1985): 29-39.
      Discusses means of estimating the direct impacts of
      new industrial development on communities in southeas-
      tern states. Impacts with respect to local labor
      markets, occupational health, employment stability, and
      energy use are discussed.

390. Goode, F.M. "The Potential for Economic Development in
      Rural Communities in the Northeast." *Journal of the
      Northeastern Agricultural Economics Council* 1, no. 2
      (October 1981): 21-28.
      Suggests that the labor costs and market conditions
      that have allegedly been responsible for the movement of
      traditional manufacturing out of the Northeast may be
      changing. This change is suggested by the recent
      economic performance in New England and by Pittsburgh's
      ability to attract firms in rapidly growing manu-
      facturing sectors.

391. Goodwin, H.L., and James R. Nelson. *Changes in Oklahoma
      Municipal Government Costs from Industrial Development
      and Growth.* Bull. B-748. Stillwater, Okla.: Agr.
      Exp. Sta., Oklahoma State University, 1979. 25 pp.
      Develops and tests econometric models (1) relating
      total operating and maintenance costs of municipal
      governments to economic and demographic characteristics
      of small rural Oklahoma towns and to particular types of
      local industrial development, and (2) identifying
      operation and maintenance costs associated with specific
      types of community services based on local economic and
      demographic characteristics.

392. Gyekye, Agyapong Boateng. "The Impact of Locational and
      Community Characteristics on the Structure of Employ-
      ment and Economic Growth in Nonmetropolitan Areas of
      the North Central Region of the United States." Ph.D.
      Dissertation. Columbus: Ohio State University, 1982.
      187 pp.
      Analyzes the impact of locational and community
      characteristics on the structure of employment and
      economic growth in nonmetropolitan areas of the North
      Central region. The results indicate that net inmigra-

tion and employment growth positively influence each other.

393. Helgeson, Delmer L., and Maurice J. Zink. *A Case Study of Rural Industrialization in Jamestown, North Dakota.* Agr. Econ. Rpt. No. 95. Fargo, N.D.: North Dakota State University, Agr. Econ. Dept., 1973. 42 pp.
     Details a case study of a rural region successful in expanding its industrial sector. The social and economic impact and acceptance of rural industrialization were examined.

394. Henry, Mark, and Kathy Lambert. "The Impact of New Industry on County Government Property Tax Revenue." *Southern Journal of Agricultural Economics* 12, no. 1 (1980): 193-97.
     Develops an alternative framework for analyzing the property tax impact of new industry. The model presented treats tax-expenditure behavior of the local public sector as a problem of maximizing community welfare subject to a budget constraint.

395. Hoffman, Randy, and Thomas L. Dobbs. *Water Use by Rural Manufacturing Firms in South Dakota.* B678. Brookings, S. Dak.: South Dakota State University, Agr. Exp. Sta., 1981. 27 pp.
     Reports results of a study designed to determine (1) water requirements of the types of manufacturing firms that have located in nonmetropolitan communities (less than 50,000 persons) of South Dakota in recent years, with emphasis on eastern South Dakota; (2) added costs to communities of supplying water and associated conveyance facilities to new manufacturing and processing firms; and (3) patterns of sharing these water supply costs between manufacturing firms and the local communities in which they reside.

396. Hoyt, Ann. "Cooperatives--Tool for Rural Revitalization." *Extension Review* 58, no. 1 (1987): 14-15.
     Reports that Wisconsin is fostering and assisting diverse cooperative businesses as one way to strengthen the state's rural agricultural and nonfarm economies. The University of Wisconsin's Center for Cooperatives provides training and technical assistance to agricultural, consumer, and worker-owned cooperatives.

397. Hudson, James F., and Brian Chapman. *Economic Analysis of the Louisiana Commercial Campground Industry.*

D.A.E. Res. Rpt. No. 603. Baton Rouge, La.: Louisiana
State University, Department of Agricultural Economics, 1982. 21 pp.
   Develops basic economic information about the commercial campground segment of the private recreation
industry in Louisiana and determines its contribution to
rural communities and the state's economy. Specifically, the authors (1) determine the overall economic state
of the commercial campground industry and provide
information concerning some of the major problems faced
by the industry, and (2) determine the direct economic
importance of the commercial campground industry to
rural communities and to the state.

398. Huskey, Lee. "Import Substitution: The Hidden Dynamic
      in the Growth of Frontier Regions." *Growth and Change*
      16, no. 4 (1985): 43-55.
   Examines the process of structural change that occurs
in frontier economies as a result of the local production of goods and services previously available only
outside the region--this is, broadly defined, the
process of import substitution. In frontier regions it
includes both the replacement of imported goods and
services and the production of goods and services that
were not previously consumed because of high import
costs. Import substitution was examined with reference
to the economy of Alaska.

399. Jackson, Randall W. "An Evaluation of Alternative
      Measures of Regional Industrial Diversification."
      Regional Studies 18, no. 2 (1984): 103-12.
   Conducts an empirical analysis of the relationship
between employment stability and four measures of
diversity for multicounty regions in Illinois. Results
indicate that the nature of the stability/diversity
relationship is swamped by the measurement and estimation techniques employed. Current diversity measures
are deemed inadequate for regional policymakers.

400. Jones, Michael G. "Industrial Parks: Their Effective-
      ness in Attracting Industry in Rural Areas." *AEDC
      Journal* 16, no. 1 (Summer 1981): 23-34.
   Attempts to determine if industrial parks in Georgia
have aided rural communities of less than 50,000
population in attracting new industry and creating jobs.
To measure success, a comparison was made between
communities with and without industrial parks.

401. Kale, Steven R. "U.S. Industrial Development Incentives
      and Manufacturing Growth during the 1970s." *Growth
      and Change* 15, no. 1 (1984): 26-34.
      Discusses manufacturing growth or decline and in-
      dustrial development incentives in the United States
      during the 1970s. The discussion focuses primarily on
      manufacturing employment changes for regions and states
      and the relationship of industrial incentives to these
      changes.

402. Klindt, T.H., B.J. Deaton, and M.R. Landes. "The
      Determinants of Wage Increases in New Manufacturing
      Plants in Rural Areas." *Southern Journal of Agricul-
      tural Economics* 13, no. 1 (1981): 83-88.
      Presents results that are generally consistent with
      the argument that individual worker, plant, and com-
      munity characteristics influence employee wage changes
      in newly located plants. The unexplained variation
      suggests the need for additional work in determining
      explanations for wage changes or in specifying ex-
      planatory variables.

403. Klindt, Thomas H., Brady J. Deaton, and Carl R.
      Siegrist, Jr. "Factors Affecting the Probability of
      New Plant Locations in Kentucky and Tennessee Non
      metropolitan Communities." *Tennessee Farm and Home
      Science* 112 (1979): 12-15.
      Presents results of a study designed to determine the
      impact of community characteristics and recruitment
      efforts on the probability of an industrial location.
      The study was based on survey data obtained from 565
      incorporated nonmetropolitan communities in Kentucky and
      Tennessee. Information was obtained by personal
      interviews with plant managers and community leaders and
      included data on community characteristics and in-
      dustrialization experiences during 1970 through 1973.

404. Krannich, Richard S., and Thomas Greider. "Personal
      Well-Being in Rapid Growth and Stable Communities:
      Multiple Indicators and Contrasting Results." *Rural
      Sociology* 49, no. 4 (1984): 541-52.
      Uses three indicators of personal well-being to
      examine differences and similarities between two groups
      of residents in a rapidly growing town and between those
      persons and residents of a community with a relatively
      stable population. Results provide evidence of disrup-
      tion on only one of the well-being indicators and also
      indicate the importance of disaggregating boom town

populations into distinct subpopulations when attempting
to assess the effects of rapid growth.

405. Kuehn, John A., and Curtis Braschler. *New Manufacturing
     Plants in the Nonmetro Ozarks Region*. Agr. Econ. Rpt.
     No. 384. Washington, D.C.: USDA, Economic Development
     Division, Economic Research Service, 1977. 33 pp.
     Examines the location of new manufacturing plants in
nonmetropolitan areas of five Ozarks states from 1967 to
1974. Most located in towns of less than 25,000
population. New plants were very diversified; 286
different industries were represented.

406. Kuehn, John A., Curtis Braschler, and J. Scott Shonk-
     wiler. "Rural Industrialization and Community Action:
     New Plant Locations Among Missouri's Small Towns."
     Journal of Community Development Society 10, no. 1
     (1979): 95-107.
     Identifies community characteristics associated with
new plant locations. The analysis focuses on new plants
that located or relocated in Missouri's nonmetropolitan
towns of less than 5,000 population during the period
1972 to 1974.

407. Kuehn, John A., Lloyd D. Bender, Bernal L. Green, and
     Herbert Hoover. *Impact of Job Development on Poverty
     in Four Developing Areas, 1970*. Agr. Econ. Rpt. No.
     225. Washington, D.C.: USDA, Economic Research
     Service, Government Printing Office, 1972. 14 pp.
     (Doc. A93.28: 225)
     Estimates the direct economic impact of job develop-
ment in new and expanded plants in four developing areas
in Arizona, Appalachian Mississippi, the Mississippi
Delta area in Arkansas, and the Ozarks area of northwestern Arkansas.

408. Kulshreshtha, Surendra N. "Short-Run Effects of An
     Inland Terminal on the Grain Handling System and Rural
     Communities: A Case Study of Weyburn." *Prairie Forum*
     7, no. 1 (1982): 69-85.
     Reports that the construction at Weyburn, Sas-
katchewan, of an inland grain terminal with a storage
capacity of one million bushels has been surrounded by
controversy since 1973. The short-term impact of the
terminal on the grain movement and on rural communities
is assessed by examining the changes in the capacity of
the elevators, population, taxable assessment, and
business services. The careful analysis of these

factors concludes that the Weyburn inland terminal, in
the short-term, has not altered the grain-handling or
rural-community systems in the region.

409.   Larson, Donald K., and Claudia K. White. *Will Employ-
       ment Growth Benefit All Households? A Case Study in
       Nine Nonmetro Kentucky Counties.* Rural Dev. Res. Rpt.
       No. 55. Washington, D.C.: USDA, Economic Research
       Service, 1986. 24 pp. (Doc. A93.41: 55)
       Indicates that overall employment growth in a rural
       area will probably not benefit all households or
       residents in that area. In a nine-county area of south
       central Kentucky, rapid employment growth between 1974
       and 1979 did create new job opportunities; however, only
       18 percent of the households had members who took
       advantage of new jobs. The employment growth also did
       not reduce the area's overall poverty level. Some
       population groups, such as households headed by women,
       remained economically disadvantaged despite the area's
       growth. Other groups, such as the elderly, maintained
       their income status by relying on public and private
       income transfer programs.

410.   Lloyd, R.C., and K.P. Wilkinson. "Community Factors in
       Rural Manufacturing Development." *Rural Sociology* 50,
       no. 1 (1985): 27-37.
       Contends that conventional theories on manufacturing
       development have paid little attention to the influence
       of community factors on the location and/or expansion of
       manufacturing firms in rural areas. This study argues
       that greater consideration must be given to these
       factors before the current economic changes impacting
       rural communities can be fully understood. The factors
       of interest are community activeness and solidarity.
       The effects of these two factors on rural manufacturing
       development in 160 nonmetropolitan communities of
       Pennsylvania are estimated in a regression analysis with
       controls for linkages between the community and larger
       economic systems.

411.   Lloyd, Robert Charles. "The Influence of Vertical and
       Horizontal Linkages on Manufacturing Employment in
       Rural Communities of Pennsylvania." Ph.D. Disserta-
       tion. University Park, Pa.: Pennsylvania State
       University, 1982. 218 pp.
       Maintains that conventional theories of industrial
       development provide an incomplete foundation for
       analyzing the location and/or expansion of manufacturing

firms in rural areas. Multiple regression was used to
analyze the relationship between fourteen community
linkages and manufacturing employment. Results reveal
that linkages do have an impact on the level of manufacturing employment found in communities of Pennsylvania.

412. Lonsdale, Richard E., and H.L. Seyler. *Nonmetropolitan
Industrialization*. New York: V.H. Winston and Sons,
1979. 196 pp.
Explores the transformation of the nonmetropolitan
industrial landscape and the impact of nonmetropolitan
industrialization. Specifically, the authors discuss
plant location (factors that encourage and discourage
plant location and characteristics of branch plants
attracted to rural areas), community satisfaction with
manufacturers, socioeconomic impacts of industrialization, migration, and household income levels. The book
closes with a discussion of coping with industrialization and implications for development policy.

413. Mathews, Michael J. "The Emergence of Business Incubators: A Local Initiative for Economic Development." Paper presented to the Community Development
Society, 28 July 1987. Available from the author at
Madison Gas and Electric Company, P. O. Box 1231,
Madison, Wisc. 53701-1231.
Points out that (1) small business is big business,
(2) incubators were originally created as a way to
address the problems of small business volatility at the
local level, (3) incubators are not being established
just for job creation any longer, (4) not all incubators
will be successful, and (5) the next evolution in this
area is the emergence of incubator networks.

414. McGowan, Anne. *Economic Development for Small Local
Governments: An Annotated Bibliography*. CPL Bib. No.
121. Chicago, Ill.: CPL Bibliography, 1983. 19 pp.
Contains forty-seven entries from the period 1979-1983
that are useful to local economic development planners
engaged in efforts to broaden their communities'
economic bases.

415. McMillan, T.E., Jr. "Why Manufacturers Choose Plant
Locations vs. Determinants of Plant Locations." *Land
Economics* 41, no. 3 (August 1965): 239-46.
Discusses some of the important factors of plant
location and how they can vary in importance to various
types of industries. McMillan stresses a continuous and

sound program of community financial control, orderly
and continuous planning, and the maintenance of a
constructive, broad-based community attitude encompassing a good business climate.

416.   MDC, Inc. *Broadening the Base of Economic Development:
       New Approaches for Rural Development*. Chapel Hill,
       N.C., 1986. 155 pp.
       Provides an in-depth look at alternatives to in-
       dustrial recruitment using recommendations from detailed
       case studies of over twenty development organizations,
       primarily in the South. Examples are given of how local
       organizations can utilize untapped rural resources and
       local markets, including markets offered by existing
       businesses and by the need for human services. A
       variety of business types are addressed.

417.   Milkove, D.L., and D.B. Weisblat. *The Effects of the
       Competitive Structure of Financial Institutions on
       Rural Bank Performance and Economic Growth*. ERS Staff
       Rpt. AGES 820226. Washington, D.C.: USDA, Economic
       Research Service, April 1982. 26 pp.
       Discovered that the competitive structure of local
       financial markets is not a factor in explaining 1973-
       1977 employment growth in a sample of 220 non-
       metropolitan counties. Loan-to-deposit ratios of
       commerical banks also failed to explain employment
       growth. The study did support the hypothesis that bank
       performance is affected by the degree of local financial
       competition. Banks participating in more competitive
       markets had higher loan-to-deposit ratios and lower net
       income-to-assets ratios.

418.   Miller, James P. "Rethinking Small Businesses as the
       Best Way to Create Rural Jobs." *Rural Development
       Perspectives* 1, no. 1 (1985): 9-12.
       Reports that, while many areas try to encourage small
       local firms as sources of new jobs, new data show that
       such firms create less than a third of new jobs and that
       they are an unreliable employment source because many
       fail within their first five years of business. More
       than half the new jobs in rural areas are created by
       branch plants of large corporations.

419.   Moriarty, Barry M. *Industrial Location and Community
       Development*. Chapel Hill, N.C.: University of North
       Carolina Press, 1980. 381 pp.

Examines locational trends in manufacturing and the
site-selection process. Moriarty also focuses on
factors related to industrial location: transportation,
labor, utilities, energy, environment, and taxation. He
then examines governmental and nongovernmental sources
of financing industry and closes with a discussion of
community development strategies.

420. Nuttal, T. *The Role of Local Authorities in Promoting*
      the Creation or Operation of Small or Medium-sized
      Firms within a General Policy of Endogenous Develop-
      ment. Strasbourg, France: Council of Europe, 1986.
      31 pp.
      Highlights activities undertaken in European countries
      to encourage the development of small and medium-sized
      enterprises.

421. Oliveira, Victor J., and John A. Kuehn. *Distribution of*
      Employment Growth in 10 Ozark Counties: A Case Study.
      Rural Dev. Res. Rpt. No. 66. Washington, D.C.: USDA,
      Economic Research Service, 1987. 33 pp.
      Reports that service industries, some manufacturing,
      and a concentration of retirees can provide a strong
      economic base for a rural area. Rapid growth of service
      businesses, especially wholesale and retail firms and
      other businesses related to tourism and recreation,
      attracted job-seekers to a ten-county area in the Ozark
      Mountains of Arkansas and Missouri during 1978-1984.
      Newcomers were better educated and held higher-paying
      jobs than long-term residents. The recreation busi-
      nesses provided increased job opportunities for youths
      but tended to pay low wages and be seasonal, based on
      tourism patterns. Manufacturing industries provided
      about a fourth of the jobs in the area, many of them
      higher paying than jobs in the service sector. The area
      also benefited from the stable incomes and buying
      patterns of retirees who made up 33 percent of the adult
      residents.

422. Organisation For Economic Co-Operation and Development
      (OECD). *Community Business Ventures and Job Creation.*
      Paris, France: OECD, 1984. 76 pp.
      Examines community business ventures, an intermediate
      form of business organization between the market economy
      and a state organization. The report examines three
      major aspects on a multinational basis: (1) types of
      community business ventures and job-creation strategies,
      (2) obstacles and aids to the development of community

business ventures, and (3) steps that could be taken to encourage community business ventures.

423. Perry, Charles S. "Industrialization, Income, and Inequality: Further Considerations." *Rural Sociology* 45, no. 1 (1980): 139-46.
      Uses regression analysis to examine changes in income and income inequality using data from 120 Kentucky counties for 1960 and 1970. Results indicate that levels of inequality in 1960 had a pronounced negative relationship with changing inequality and that levels of income and industrialization, respectively, had sig-nificant negative and positive effects. Change in neither income nor industrialization significantly affected change in inequality.

424. Plaut, Thomas R., and Joseph E. Pluta. "Business Climate, Taxes and Expenditures, and State Industrial Growth in the United States." *Southern Economic Journal* 50, no. 1 (1983): 99-119.
      Tests the effect of four groups of variables (acces-sibility to markets, cost and availability of factors of production, climate and environment, and business climate and state and local taxes and expenditures) on three separate measures of industrial growth, which measure overall, labor-intensive, and capital-intensive growth.

425. Premus, Robert. "Attracting High-Tech Industry and Jobs: An Assessment of State Practices." *Financing Economic Development in the 1980s: Issues and Trends* (item 503), pp. 55-71.
      Examines the leading issues involved in creating a climate for innovation and high-technology growth at the regional level. The experiences of Utah, North Caro-lina, and Pennsylvania in their attempts to create a better climate for entrepreneurship and innovation are examined. The discussion concludes with an overall assessment of the state and local high-technology movement and its implications for national public policy.

426. President's Economic Adjustment Committee. *Summary of Completed Military Base Economic Adjustment Projects: 1961-1981, 10 Years of Civilian Reuse.* Washington, D.C.: U.S. Department of Defense, Office of Economic Adjustment, 1981. 25 pp.

Reports on the results of economic adjustment assistance that has been provided to alleviate local impacts of defense program changes. This summary of 94 military-base, economic-adjustment projects identifies the military and civilian job losses; the replacement of civilian jobs; the principal industrial, commercial, and public reuse activities; and the individual community contacts who can provide additional information.

427. Preston, Richard, ed. *Principles of Industrial Development*. 3d ed., rev. South Hamilton, Maine: AIDC Education Foundation, 1981. 156 pp.
    Designed to instruct local leadership and the public about the broad principles of industrial development through the use of the book and the audiovisual instruction series, which is also available. Subjects include facility planning, forming an industrial development team, data compilation, dealing with existing industry, industrial sites, speculative buildings, project financing, promotion, and transportation.

428. Rasmussen, David W., Marc Bendick, Jr., and Larry C. Ledebur. "A Methodology for Selecting Economic Development Incentives." *Growth and Change* 15, no. 1 (1984): 18-25.
    Presents a rigorous cost-minimization approach to part of the problem of evaluating the effectiveness of economic development incentives, thereby avoiding the more intractable measurement of the firm's behavioral response. The authors examine public bodies that have decided to aid firms in order to achieve some public purpose (e.g., job creation or tax revenue generation). The analysis seeks to discover the form of aid that will minimize the public cost of a given level of assistance to the firm.

429. Ratner, Shanna, and Peter Ide. *Strategies For Community Economic Development Through Natural Resource Use in Northern New York*. A.E. Res. 85-10. Ithaca, N.Y.: Cornell University, Department of Agricultural Economics, 1985. 38 pp.
    Provides an alternative framework for assessing the economic potential of small- to medium-scale agricultural and natural resource-related endeavors for improving the economic climate in northern New York and, specifically, presents area residents and development professionals with examples of innovative solutions to the problem of stimulating economic progress in isolated

rural regions. The authors have identified, reviewed, and analyzed initiatives in resource-based community economic development recently introduced in rural America, Canada, and Great Britain.

430. Rogers, David L., Brian F. Pendleton, Willis J. Goudy, and Robert O. Richards. "Industrialization, Income Benefits, and the Rural Community." *Rural Sociology* 43, no. 2 (1978): 250-61.
      Examines the equality of individual income distribution for all residents of Iowa towns of 2,500 to 10,000. A positive, but weak, relationship was observed between the percentage of the community's labor force employed in manufacturing and the equality of income distribution. In general, these authors conclude that the relationship between changes in manufacturing activity and changes in income distribution may be inconsequential in smaller towns that do not experience large changes in manufacturing activity.

431. Ryan, Mary Jean. *Small Business Incubators: New Directions in Economic Development*. Washington, D.C.: U.S. Small Business Administration, Office of Private Sector Initiatives, 1986. 33 pp.
      Is a guidebook and workbook for exploring the feasibility of establishing a business incubator. Financing an incubator and steps for successful market research and implementation are discussed.

432. Sampson, Stephanie, ed. *Economic Development Through Exports: A Guide to Local Action*. Washington, D.C.: National Council for Urban Economic Development, 1982. 200 pp.
      Helps practitioners assess export potential of their business community and design programs to make exporting part of a business retention and expansion strategy. The urban focus can also be useful to regional planners.

433. Schaub, James D., and Victor J. Oliveira. *Distribution of Employment Growth in 10 Georgia Counties: A Case Study*. Rural Dev. Res. Rpt. No. 53. Washington, D.C.: USDA, Economic Research Service, 1985. 39 pp. (Doc. A93.41: 53)
      Reports that rapid economic growth in a ten-county rural area in south Georgia during 1976-1981 favored employment of whites, men, and immigrants. They earned higher average weekly salaries than blacks, women, and long-term residents. This study of growth in a mixed

manufacturing- and agricultural-based economy flows from
a research project on the impacts of economic expansion
in nonmetropolitan economies with different industrial
bases. The Georgia area's job growth was greatest in
the trade and services sectors.

* Simon, William, and John H. Gagnon. "The Decline and
    Fall of the Small Town." *The Community: A Comparative
    Perspective.* Cited above as item 140.

434. Smith, E.D., and T.H. Klindt. *Industrial Location and
    Growth in Submetro Tennessee and Kentucky Communities.*
    Southern Cooperative Series Bulletin, June 1981. 69
    pp.
    Compiles the component parts of a Southern Regional
    Project. In general, the research indicated that some
    nonmetropolitan communities have locational and other
    nonmodifiable disadvantages in attracting new in-
    dustries. However, statistical evidence indicates that
    most of these disadvantages could be counteracted by
    effective community action programs. Moreover, it was
    found that the market for manufacturing industry
    locations is highly imperfect. However, it appears to
    be one that is more efficient in the higher technology,
    male-labor-oriented industries with high value added per
    worker.

435. Smith, Eldon D., Brady Deaton, and David Kelch. "Cost-
    Effective Programs of Rural Community Industrializa-
    tion." *Journal of Community Development Society* 11,
    no. 1 (1980): 113-23.
    Provides information about industrial potentials for
    rural communities and helps to identify effective
    industrial development program directions. Data are
    from a study of 565 incorporated nonmetropolitan
    communities in Kentucky and Tennessee for the period
    1970-1973.

436. Smith, Gary W., David B. Willis, and Bruce A. Weber.
    *The Aging Population, Retirement Income, and the Local
    Economy.* WRDC 36. Corvallis, Ore.: Oregon State
    University, Western Rural Development Center, 1987.
    15 pp.
    Examines the increasing economic importance of the
    expanding elderly population and the growth of transfer
    payment incomes, and explores the implications of these
    changes for rural communities. The authors contend that
    the incomes of a growing retirement population can be

viewed as a new and emerging basic industry in some
rural areas.

437.   Smith, Stephen M.   "Diversifying Small Town Economies
       with Nonmanufacturing Industries." *Rural Development
       Perspectives* 2 (October 1985): 18-22.
       Describes the role of service industries in the
       economic development plan for a small town or rural
       area, based on surveys administered in Wisconsin.   Data
       are given on the export orientation of service-oriented
       businesses in nonmetropolitan communities and on the
       relative importance of traditional market factors.

438.   Smith, Stephen M.   "Export Orientation of Nonmanufactur-
       ing Businesses in Nonmetropolitan Communities."
       American Journal of Agricultural Economics 66, no. 2
       (1984): 145-55.
       Argues that nonmanufacturing firms are also a viable
       means to expand the economic base of rural communities.
       Community and firm characteristics are examined by
       regression analysis to determine factors associated with
       higher export levels.

439.   Smith, Stephen M., and David L. Barkley.   "Labor Force
       Characteristics of 'High Tech' vs. 'Low Tech' Manufac-
       turing in Nonmetropolitan Counties in the West."
       Journal of the Community Development Society 19
       (1988): in press.
       Compares the labor force characteristics of high-
       technology and traditional (low-technology) manufactur-
       ing firms in nonmetropolitan counties.   The main
       objectives are to (1) provide a further test of the
       product-profit cycle hypothesis for high-technology
       manufacturing; (2) determine if high- and low-technology
       manufacturers provide different employment opportunities
       for nonmetropolitan residents; and (3) provide citizens
       and policymakers with more specific information on which
       to base job development programs and expected impacts.

440.   Smith, Stephen M., and Glen C. Pulver.   "Nonmanu-
       facturing Business as a Growth Alternative In Non-
       metropolitan Areas." *Journal of the Community
       Development Society* 12, no. 1 (1981): 33-47.
       Provides information on the nonmanufacturing business
       sector and recommends it as an alternative to small
       towns trying to provide more employment opportunities.
       Four characteristics of these businesses are described:
       size of businesses as measured by employment, level of

linkages to the local economy, types of ownership structure, and factors that favor or hinder location and operation in nonmetropolitan communities.

441. Smith, Stephen M., and Glen C. Pulver. *Characteristics of Nonmanufacturing Businesses in Nonmetropolitan Wisconsin*. R2879. Madison, Wisc.: University of Wisconsin, College of Agricultural and Life Sciences Research Division, 1980.

    Presents a description of selected characteristics of nonmanufacturing businesses in nonmetropolitan counties of Wisconsin, based upon a 1976 survey of 385 firms. The businesses studied do not necessarily depend upon local population and income levels for their markets, and are felt to have the same potential to contribute to a community's economic and employment goals as manufacturing. The main characteristics of nonmanufacturing businesses examined are (1) types of businesses located in nonmetropolitan areas; (2) size of businesses measured by employment and expenditures; (3) level of linkages to the local economy via local expenditures and sales; (4) types of ownership structure and degree of nonlocal ownership; and (5) factors that most affect location decisions and operating efficiency.

442. Stevens, J.B., K.L. Bunch, and B.M. Soth. *New Shops on Maine Street: A Growth Industry*. Corvallis, Ore.: Oregon State University, Agr. Exp. Sta., May 1981. 38 pp.

    Considers the possibility that self-employment by recent inmigrants may have expanded the net export base in Jackson County. However, only about 15 percent of the new inmigrant firms exported (outside the county) more than they imported; these firms combined fabrication of a product with wholesaling and/or retailing functions. The remainder of the firms compete with existing firms for existing markets and for the anticipated growth of these markets. Although these firms may benefit local consumers by providing price and service competition, they operate within rather than expanding the net export base of the community.

443. Stevens, Joe B., and Linda P. Owen. "Migration and Employment Change: Some New Evidence and New Considerations." *Western Journal of Agricultural Economics* 7, no. 2 (1982): 155-62.

    Uses data from selected counties in the Pacific Northwest from 1965 to 1970 to refute the argument that

jobs follow people. The authors conclude that the
problem may become increasingly difficult to model if
the desire for nonmarket goods, rather than income gain,
continues to evolve as a major reason for migration.

444. Stoevener, Herbert H., and Roger G. Kraynick. "On
      Augmenting Community Economic Performance by New or
      Continuing Irrigation Developments." *American Journal
      of Agricultural Economics* 61, no. 5 (1979): 1115-23.
      Examines the nature and extent of regional irrigation
development impacts. The authors identify some of the
major policy issues involved, classify relevant empirical studies on this subject, and make some suggestions
for research approaches.

445. Summers, Gene F., and Kristi Branch. "Economic Develop-
      ment and Community Social Change." *Annual Review of
      Sociology* 10 (1984): 141-66.
      Extracts and reviews what has been learned from
studies of communities coping with rural industrialization and natural resource development, especially
large-scale projects. Particular attention is given to
changes in employment patterns, income, population,
agriculture, local businesses, and public sector costs
and revenues. The findings reveal an underlying tension
between the free movement of capital, on the one hand,
and community stability and worker welfare, on the other
hand. The authors conclude that local social changes
are integral elements of external processes of economic
development. They may be understood by directing
attention to the spatial patterns of social, economic,
and political inequality and to the mechanisms that
generate and sustain unevenness.

446. Summers, Gene F., Sharon D. Evans, Frank Clemente, E.M.
      Beck, and Jon Minkoff. *Industrial Invasion of
      Nonmetropolitan America: A Quarter Century of Ex-
      periences*. New York: Praeger Publishers, 1976. 231
      pp.
      Attempts to assess the validity of the view that the
location of industry in small cities, towns, and rural
areas is an important tool for solving the twin problems
of rural poverty and urban crisis. Case studies of
industrial plants located in nonmetropolitan areas
provide the data base for the study. A total of 186
case study documents provided information for assessing
the impact of industrial development on (1) population
dynamics, (2) the private sector, (3) the public sector,

and (4) the quality of individual well-being in the host
communities.

447. Sweet, Morris L. "How Corporations View British
      Facility Controls." *Area Development* 12 (April 1977):
      16, 40, 42, 44.
      Relates the experiences of companies establishing
facilities in the United Kingdom under the Industrial
Development Certificate system, which seeks to move
development away from prosperous to depressed regions by
means of locational controls on industries.

448. Sweet, Morris L. "Industrial Location Policy: Western
      European Precedents for Aiding U.S. Impacted Regions."
      Urbanism Past and Present 7 (Winter 1978-79): 1-12.
      Examines legislation in Western Europe concerning the
location of new industries and facilities. In these
nations, industry is limited in selecting locations for
new plants, and a company may not relocate without the
permission of the government. The applicability of
these policies is discussed in terms of aiding declining
regions, especially in the Northeast United States.

449. Temali, Mihailo, and Candace Campbell. *Business
      Incubator Profiles: A National Survey*. Minneapolis,
      Minn.: Hubert H. Humphrey Institute, 1984. 130 pp.
      Profiles fifty business incubators sponsored by
public, nonprofit, university, and private organizations. The authors highlight lessons learned by
developers of these facilities and detail the size,
method of financing, range of services offered, and jobs
created in each. Incubators in several states are
represented.

450. Thoss, Rainer, and Heiner Kleinschneider. "Alternative
      Strategies to Full Employment in a Regional Labor
      Market." *Annals of Regional Science* 17, no. 1 (1983):
      56-68.
      Addresses the development of employment and manpower
in Borken County, situated in the Federal Republic of
Germany close to the Dutch border. The authors discuss
alternative strategies on the labor demand and supply
sides, which may serve to reach full employment. The
main objective is to estimate the sectoral structure of
labor demand and the professional structure of labor
supply, which in combination would lead to full employment by 1990. Alternative optimizations show that an
overall increase of employment as well as an increased

professional flexibility of the labor force are necessary to reach the employment objective.

451. U.S. Department of Commerce. *Creating Jobs by Creating
     New Business Incubators*. Washington, D.C.: Economic
     Development Administration, 1985. Available from the
     National Council for Urban Economic Development. 71
     pp.
     Provides an overview of the relative success of
     business incubators based on survey responses from
     forty-six incubators, some of which are in smaller urban
     settings. Topics include assessing feasibility,
     facility operating characteristics, services provided,
     staffing and management, and economic development
     outcomes from incubators.

452. van Willigen, John, Thomas A. Arcury, and Robert G.
     Cromley. "Tobacco Men and Factory Hands: The Effects
     of Migration Turnaround and Decentralized In-
     dustrialization on the Social Lives of Older People in
     a Rural Kentucky County." *Human Organization* 44
     (Spring 1985): 50-57.
     Examines the effects of migration turnaround and
     industrial dispersion on the social lives of older
     people in a rural Kentucky county, which until recently,
     was declining in population. The authors found a
     decrease in social density, age integration, and
     neighborhood cooperation.

453. Vaughan, Roger J., and Robert Pollard. "Small Business
     and Economic Development." *Financing Economic
     Development in the 1980s: Issues and Trends* (item
     503), pp. 122-138.
     Explores the evidence that small businesses are major
     sources of employment growth and innovation, suggests
     that economic development can best be viewed as an
     "entrepreneurial process," and considers the contribu-
     tion of small business to this process. The chapter
     concludes by recommending that economic development
     policy should foster entrepreneurship in firms of any
     size and not provide special privileges to firms merely
     because they are small.

454. Wadsworth, H.A., and J.M. Conrad. *Impact of a New
     Industry on a Rural Community*. Res. Bull. No. 811.
     Lafayette, Indiana: Purdue University, July 1966. 14
     pp.

Presents the results of a case study analysis of
Linton, Indiana, that received limited employment and
income benefits from a new industrial plant. Net gain
in income was lower due to nonresident workers exporting
their wages, former commuters who returned to Linton to
work, higher than average tendencies to save, and the
retirement of old debts faster than new ones were
assumed.

455. Wadsworth, H.A., and J.M. Conrad. "Leakages Reducing
Employment and Income Multipliers in Labor-Surplus
Rural Areas." *Journal of Farm Economics* 47 (1965):
1197-1202.
Examines the differences in income multipliers in
areas of labor surplus and shortage when new industry is
added to the area. Leakages, which reduce the size of
the multiplier, are identified and discussed.

456. Wagner, Kenneth C. *Economic Development Manual.*
Jackson, Miss.: University Press of Mississippi, 1978.
158 pp.
Provides information on recruiting new business to a
Mississippi community. Chapters discuss frequent errors
in the development effort, determining needs and goals,
dealing with individuals resistant to change, securing
good industrial sites, community appearance, and
handling industrial prospects.

457. Wallace, L.T. *Factors Affecting Industrial Location in
Southern Indiana 1955-1958.* Res. Bull 724. La-
fayette, Ind.: Purdue University, 1961. 23 pp.
Identifies factors that affected the location of 72
new industrial plants that located in southern Indiana
from January 1955 through December 1958. Wallace
develops an approach to industrial location that
considers the role of the community as a location
influence and presents some empirical evidence il-
lustrating the effectiveness of community action in
influencing industrialization in southern Indiana.

458. Walton, Jeff, Steve Griesert, and Kevin Locke. "A Tale
of Three Cities: Maple Plain, Faribault, and Hopkins."
Minnesota Cities 70 (1985): 11-14.
Summarizes experiences of three Minnesota cities in
attracting and keeping businesses in their communities.
The authors are the development directors of the towns,
which range in population from 1,421 to 16,241.

459. Wasylenko, Michael. "The Effect of Business Climate on
      Employment Growth: A Review of the Evidence."
      *Financing Economic Development in the 1980s: Issues
      and Trends* (item 503), pp. 34-54.
      Analyzes the possible indirect effects of taxes on
      locational decisions of both manufacturing and non-
      manufacturing industries.

460. Weinberg, Mark L. "Business Incubators Give New Firms
      in Rural Areas a Head Start." *Rural Development
      Perspectives* 3 (February 1987): 6-10.
      Points out that, while four out of five new businesses
      fail within their first four years, business incubators
      sponsored by local governments or other groups can help
      improve those odds. Incubators provide shared office
      services and rental space at below-market costs.

461. Williams, James, Andrew Sofranko, and Brenda Root.
      "Change Agents and Industrial Development in Small
      Towns." *Journal of the Community Development Society*
      8, no. 1 (1977): 19-29.
      Examines data from 162 small communities in Illinois
      to determine what factors differentiate the communities
      acquiring new firms from those not acquiring them. The
      contrasting ecological and social action explanations
      and findings are discussed in terms of their implica-
      tions for the role of the community development special-
      ist in industrial development efforts.

Financing Revitalization

462. Back, W.B. "Estimating Contributions of Natural
      Resource Investments to Objectives in Regional
      Economic Development." *American Journal of Agricul-
      tural Economics* 51 (1969): 1442-48.
      Assesses the status of methods for estimating con-
      tributions of federal water resource development
      projects with respect to regional economic objectives.

463. Baker, John A. *A Guide to Federal Programs for Rural
      Development*. 4th rev. ed. Washington, D.C.: USDA,
      Rural Development Service, March 1975. 346 pp. (Doc.
      A102.8: F31)
      Prepared as a reference handbook for local leaders in
      rural communities who want to identify federal programs
      for rural development. Topics covered are jobs,

business, and industry; community facilities; community
functions and services; housing; and planning and
coordination. Individual programs are summarized, and
some are cross referenced.

464. Barker, Michael, ed. *Financing State and Local Economic
Development*. Durham, N.C.: Duke Press Policy Studies,
1983. 480 pp.
Discusses various innovations in development finance,
pension funds and economic renewal, venture capital, and
banking. Authors examine both private and public
financing of small businesses.

465. Barkley, David L., and Peter E. Helander. "Commercial
Bank Loans and Non-Metropolitan Economic Activity: A
Question of Causality." *The Review of Regional
Studies* 15 (1985): 26-32.
Uses the Granger test for causality, applied to 1975-
1980 loan and retail sales data for twenty-seven
nonmetropolitan Arizona communities, to determine if
banks have played an active or passive role in community
development. Regression results for Arizona indicate
that bank lending was sensitive to past local economic
activity. No statistical evidence was found to indicate
that bank lending leads local economic development.

466. Barkley, David L., Cindy Mellon, and Glenn T. Potts.
"Effects of Banking Structure on the Allocation of
Credit to Nonmetropolitan Communities." *Western
Journal of Agricultural Economics* 9, no. 2 (1984):
283-92.
Reports that recent and proposed legislative changes
encourage increases in multioffice banking activity.
The authors compare the allocation of credit to nonmetropolitan communities in a branch-banking state
(Arizona) to that in a unit-banking/holding-company
state (Colorado). Rapidly growing nonmetropolitan areas
have experienced increased lending activity under
statewide branching relative to unit banking. Rural
communities, which experienced slow or negative growth,
had lower loan-to-deposit ratios under branch banking
than might have existed under unit banking. Therefore,
conversion to branch banking may result in a realloca-
tion of loanable funds within nonmetropolitan areas.

467. Barrows, Richard L., and Daniel W. Bromley. "Employment
Impacts of the Economic Development Administration's

Public Works Program." *American Journal of Agricultural Economics* 57 (1975): 46-54.

Assesses the goal of the Economic Development Administration's Public Works Program to create jobs and attract industry. The project had less employment impact in large urban regions than in less populated areas. The authors conclude that the growth center strategy for allocating development funds is not the best approach for this program and that agencies should consider several approaches for allocating funds and assess their impacts early.

468. Barton, Michael B., and James D. Vitarello. "Comptroller's Programs Encourage Public/Private Community Development Partnership." *Journal of Housing* 37, May (1980): 262-67.

Reports that community reinvestment and revitalization are no longer the exclusive concern of the traditional federal agencies (e.g., Economic Development Administration). Rather, the four federal financial regulatory agencies (the Office of the Comptroller of the Currency, the Federal Deposit Insurance Corporation, the Federal Reserve Board, and the Federal Home Loan Bank Board) have begun to assume a significant role in defining issues and strategies relating to the role that financial institutions play in reinvestment activities.

469. Bearse, Peter J., ed. *Mobilizing Capital: Program Innovation and the Changing Public/Private Interface in Development Finance.* New York: Elsevier Science Publishing, 1982. 478 pp.

Concentrates on (1) the role of capital in the economic development of U.S. regions, (2) the government as an investor (public entrepreneurship and program innovations), and (3) the public-private relationship in development finance.

470. Beaumont, Enid F., and Harold A. Hovey. "State, Local, and Federal Economic Development Policies: New Federal Patterns, Chaos, or What?" *Public Administration Review* 45 (March/April 1985): 327-32.

Points out that increasing emphasis on economic development policies by state and local governments, coupled with potential changes in federal tax and spending strategies, provide considerable potential for conflict. Industrial revenue bonds and tax-exempt financing of infrastructure are threatened by potential changes in federal tax law. In addition, local develop-

ment efforts have depended heavily on financing from
federal programs, such as community development block
grants and urban development action grants--programs
potentially threatened by attempts to cut the federal
deficit.

471. Boyles, Harlan E., and A. John Vogt. "Farmers Home
Administration Financing of Community Facilities in
North Carolina." *Popular Government* 47 (1981): 14-22.
Summarizes the history of the Farmers Home Administration (FmHA) and its present major programs and then
describes its community facility programs in North
Carolina. The authors examine the magnitude and growth
of these programs in the state, the different types of
facilities built or acquired under the community
facilities programs, eligibility requirements, distribution of funds by county, and different views about
FmHA's community facility programs in North Carolina.

472. Cameron, Gordon C. *Regional Economic Development.*
Washington, D.C.: Resources for the Future, Inc.,
1970. Distributed by Johns Hopkins University Press,
Baltimore, Md. 161 pp.
Reviews the argument for federal involvement in
regional economic development and discusses the proposed
benefits of a growth-center policy, and federal legislation and program implementation of the Economic Development Administration.

473. Daniels, Belden Hull, and Michael Kieschnick. *Development Finance: A Primer for Policymakers.* Part I: *What
Government Finance Programs Can--And Cannot--Do.* Part
II: *Essential Elements of a National Development
Finance System.* Part III: *A Critique of the Administration's Current Development Finance Proposals.*
Washington, D.C.: The National Rural Center, 1978.
131 pp. total.
Examines the potential of government-sponsored
development banking programs and institutions for
improving the economies of poor communities in both
urban and rural areas. The series is an attempt to
discuss how certain failings in the working of America's
capital markets may produce uneven patterns of economic
development. The ways government policies and programs
should, and should not, be structured to deal with the
problems resulting from private investment behavior are
also examined.

474. Deaton, B.J. *Industrial Site Development Considerations
      for Rural Communities.* Blacksburg, Va.: Virginia
      Polytechnic Institute and State University, Coopera-
      tive Extension Service, March 1979, pp. 1-3.
           Suggests that Virginia's rural communities need to
      reassess their economic development strategies in the
      face of current budget constraints. Federal funds from
      the Economic Development Administration and the Farmers
      Home Administration are important sources of financial
      support for developing water and sewage facilities and
      industrial parks.

475. Dreese, G. Richard. *Banks, Bankers and Economic Growth
      in Appalachia.* Series 73, no. 8-10. Morgantown,
      W.Va.: Office of Research and Development, Appalachian
      Center, West Virginia University, 1973. 135 pp.
           Analyzes the role that bankers and banks have played
      in the economic growth and development of selected
      Appalachian counties. Data were collected from twenty
      growth counties, and significant factors explaining the
      role of banks in the growth process were isolated.
      Dreese then attempts to determine if specific banking
      factors in growth regions can be manipulated to stimu-
      late similar growth in declining areas.

476. Fisher, Peter S. "The Role of the Public Sector in
      Local Development Finance: Evaluating Alternative
      Institutional Arrangements." *Journal of Economic
      Issues* 17, no. 1 (1983): 133-53.
           Develops a framework for evaluating alternative
      economic institutions and applies the framework to
      various arrangements for financing housing and local
      economic development. Two specific institutional
      arrangements are examined: government regulation of
      private banks and creation of publicly owned banks.

477. Flowers, George A., Jr., Jerome S. Legge, Jr., Paul E.
      Radford, and David H. Wiltsee. "Targeting Funds for
      Economic Development in Rural Georgia: The Experience
      of the Georgia Department of Community Affairs."
      Public Administration Forum 41 (1981): 485-88.
           Presents the experiences of a state agency with
      targeting FmHA business and industry loan guarantee
      funds to economically distressed areas. The intent is
      to offer guidance to practitioners in other states who
      are responsible for developing and applying measures of
      local economic distress.

478. Green, R.E., and B.J. Reed. "Small Cities Need Grants Management Capacity." *Rural Development Perspectives* RDP-4 (September 1981): 28-30.
Discusses results of a study of the developmental needs of small cities and information regarding their ability to function successfully within the federal grants system.

479. Herzik, Eric B., and John P. Pelissero. "Decentralization, Redistribution and Community Development: A Reassessment of the Small Cities CDBG Program." *Public Administration Review* 46 (January/February 1986): 31-36.
Analyzes the small cities portion of the Community Development Block Grant (CDBG) program and focuses on the proposition that decentralization weakens the redistributive character of policy allocation. Also analyzed is the use of single-purpose and multipurpose grants by the Department of Housing and Urban Development and by the states.

480. Hirsch, Werner Z. *The Economics of State and Local Government*. New York: McGraw-Hill Book Company, 1970. 333 pp.
Discusses the demand for state and local government services, user charges, tax analysis and instruments, intergovernmental fiscal relations, state and local government production and costs, regulation, budgeting, and application of some analytic tools to major policy concerns.

481. Horne, James, Luther Tweeten, and David Holland. "Alternative Criteria for Guiding the Selection of Economically Depressed Areas for Special Funding." *The Annals of Regional Science* 8, no. 3 (1974): 111-22.
Examines the advantages and disadvantages of actual and proposed criteria for allocating Economic Development Administration aid to redevelopment areas. The authors conclude that underemployment rather than unemployment is a better indicator of both underutilized labor and economic need.

482. Isserman, Andrew M. "The Allocation of Funds to Small Cities Under the Community Development Block Grant Program." *American Planning Association Journal* 47 (1981): 3-24.

Reports that a uniform point system is used by Housing and Urban Development area offices to determine which small city applicants (including suburbs and rural towns) are to receive funds under the Community Development Block Grant (CDBG) program. This evaluation of the point system, based on data for twenty-five states, indicates that (1) small cities as a group receive considerably less CDBG funding relative to their need than do larger cities and urban counties, (2) tremendous variations exist in the intensity of competition across states, (3) need plays a relatively unimportant role in determining which applicants are funded, (4) the discretionary power of the area offices is the dominant factor in funding decisions, and (5) community flexibility in project design is severely constrained by the point system.

483. Janssen, Larry L., and Paul H. Gessaman. *Businessmen's Funding Sources, Use of Credit and Assessment of Credit System Adequacy in Two Regions of Rural Nebraska.* Rpt. 65. Lincoln, Nebr.: University of Nebraska, Department of Agricultural Economics, 1976. 40 pp.
Analyzes data from a sample of sixty-seven businessmen in selected municipalities of two rural Nebraska regions to determine funding sources for business operations, credit usage, and perceptions of credit system adequacy. Most respondents from both regions used credit as a source of the funds for business operations, but only one-third reported that credit supplied more than 25 percent of funds used. The primary use of credit was for the purchase of inventory, and commercial banks were the most frequently reported credit source.

484. Klindt, T.H., G.F. Smith, and D.K. Wagoner. "The Economic Impact of Public Investment Expenditures in a Rural Economy." *Municipal Management* 3, no. 3 (1981): 156-60.
Traces the expenditure of grant and loan funds to a small rural community through contractors and sub-contractors. Few of the expenditures found their way into the community's economy even though many of the funding agencies requested efforts to make needed expenditures within the target area. The authors believe the results should serve to temper optimism about the prospects for alleviating chronic economic ills in small economies even on a short-term basis with the infusion of nonspecific grant and loan funds.

485. McDonald, Robert L., and Daniel R. Siegel. "Investment and the Valuation of Firms When There is an Option to Shut Down." *International Economic Review* 26, no. 2 (1985): 331-49.
Develops and studies a methodology for valuing risky investment projects when there is an option to temporarily shutdown production when variable costs exceed operating revenues. The firm is assumed to be a risk-neutral, price-taking profit-maximizer owned by risk-averse investors.

486. Morgan, David R., and Robert E. England. "The Small Cities Block Grant Program: An Assessment of Programmatic Change Under State Control." *Public Administration Review* 44 (November 1984): 477-82.
Focuses on the small cities Community Development Block Grant program before and after state takeover. Preliminary evidence from national data and from a more detailed study of one state shows that a state-managed small cities block grant program is likely to spread funds widely and to emphasize public works projects rather than housing rehabilitation and community services.

487. Nelson, James, and Luther Tweeten. "Subsidized Labor Mobility--An Alternative Use of Development Funds." *The Annals of Regional Science* 7, no. 1 (1973): 57-66.
Estimates the rates of return on public funds used to promote labor mobility. The authors examine the development alternative of bringing laborers to areas of industry demand rather than using incentives to bring industry to areas of excess labor supply.

488. Nenno, Mary K. "Community Development Block Grants: An Overview of the First Five Years." *Journal of Housing* 37 (August 1980): 35-42.
Reviews the first five years of experience in implementing the community development block grant (CDBG) program, first adopted in 1974. The author addresses the question, How has the CDBG program developed and where is it headed? The CDBG funds are found to be central to many comprehensive local community development efforts.

489. Newlin, Larry, ed. *Resource Guide for Rural Development: Handbook for Accessing Government and Private Funding Sources.* Washington, D.C.: National Rural Center, 1978. 149 pp.

Identifies and describes federal financial assistance
by agency, state assistance, foundation assistance,
church resources, and other private sector resources.

490. Palumbo, George, and Seymour Sacks. *Rural Governments
in the Municipal Bond Market.* Staff Rpt. No. AGES
870510. Washington, D.C.: USDA, Economic Research
Service, Agriculture and Rural Economy Division, 1987.
40 pp.
Uses 1982 municipal bond sales data matched with 1980
Census of Population data to examine the characteristics
of municipal bonds categorized according to the rural
percentage of the issuing government's population. Few
instances of a simple linear relationship between key
bond variables and rurality were found.

491. Perlman, Konrad J. "New CD Regulations Make Planning
Vital." *Journal of Housing* 37 (January 1980): 30-32.
Reports that the Department of Housing and Urban
Development's regulations for community development
block grant applications pose challenges to city
planners and public administrators to improve the
planning process and make more effective use of block
grant funds. The guidelines for FY 1980 require that
cities justify the use of funds on the basis of citywide
priorities.

492. Peterson, John E. "Innovative Approaches to the Capital
Markets for Public Borrowers." *Financing Economic
Development in the 1980s: Issues and Trends* (item
503), pp. 139-61.
Provides a concise analysis of the innovations that
have been occurring in the rapidly changing arena of
public capital facility financing. The tax-exempt
market and other so-called "nondebt" sources of capital
funds (such as leasing and various forms of public-
private financing) have been recruited for financing
many new activities in recent years. Governments have
found their mission encompassing such new uses of funds
as home mortgages, student loans, and industrial and
commercial facilities. While such uses are controversial and under continual assault from the U.S. Treasury,
in most cases these nontraditional types of financing
have been the breeding grounds for innovative techniques.

493. Pryde, Paul L., Jr. "Use of Existing Assets to Fund New
Development." *Public Management* 67 (1985): 13-14.

Reports that cutbacks in federal development assistance have forced many communities to look for alternative ways to finance local economic development
projects. The author briefly describes two ways in
which cities can use existing, and often underutilized,
assets to generate private investment for local job- and
tax-creating ventures: (1) recycling development loans
and (2) funding development deposits with pension
assets.

494. Sidor, John. "State Community Development Block Grants
Require Diversity of Local Program Responses."
Journal of Housing 38 (October 1981): 484-88.
Reviews key features of the federal community development block grant program, enacted in 1981. The author
concludes that in order to utilize the new program most
effectively states must give attention to setting
articulate goals, establishing clear objectives and
priorities, and moving state resources toward those
objectives in a patterned and sensitive way.

495. Siegel, Beth, Peter Kwass, and Andrew Reamer. *Financial
Deregulation: New Opportunities for Rural Economic
Development*. Washington, D.C.: National Center for
Policy Alternatives, 1986. 180 pp.
Discusses the risks and opportunities in the fundamen-
tal changes of the federal financial system. The
authors recommend regulatory tools that can be created
by state legislatures and used by financial regulators
and community groups to counter destabilizing effects of
a less restrictive financial environment. The purpose
and design of several models of new financial institutions that are community-oriented are discussed.

496. Smith, Gary W., David B. Willis, and Bruce A. Weber.
*Transfer Payments, The Aging Population, and the
Changing Structure of the Oregon and Washington
Economies*. WRDC Paper #30. Corvallis, Ore.: Oregon
State University, Western Rural Development Center,
1986. 57 pp. plus appendix.
Explores the impacts of an expanding elderly population and the growth of transfer payment incomes in the
Oregon and Washington economies. First, the evidence
documenting these two socioeconomic trends is examined;
second, the major national transfer payment programs are
reviewed; third, the importance, structure, and growth
of transfer payment income in the Oregon and Washington
economies is analyzed; and, finally, the implications of

these trends for local development and public policy are discussed.

497.   Stinson, T.F.   "Overcoming Impacts of Growth on Local Government Finance." *Rural Development Perspectives* 4 (September 1981): 12-19.
       Overviews existing methods of raising revenues and providing services to help community leaders minimize the fiscal impacts of growth.

498.   Stinson, Thomas F. *The Effects of Taxes and Public Financing Programs on Local Industrial Development.* Agr. Econ. Rpt. No. 133. Washington, D.C.: USDA, Economic Research Service, Government Printing Office, 1968. 24 pp. (Doc. A93.28: 133)
       Summarizes the results and conclusions of a number of studies on local tax concessions and public industrial financing programs used for rural economic development.

499.   Stinson, Thomas F. *Financing Industrial Development Through State and Local Governments.* Agr. Econ. Rpt. No. 128. Washington, D.C.: USDA, Economic Research Service, Government Printing Office, 1967. 14 pp. (Doc 93.28: 128/2)
       Provides basic information about some of the ways states can provide financial assistance to new firms and to firms that want to expand or relocate. Local bond issues, industrial finance authorities, and loan guarantee plans are discussed.

500.   Summers, Gene F., and Thomas A. Hirschl. "Capturing Cash Transfer Payments and Community Economic Development." *Journal of the Community Development Society* 16, no. 2 (1985): 121-32.
       Examines the relationship between community economic development and transfer payments. Transfer payments consist mainly of government retirement program and investment income such as rents, dividends, and interest. Studies show that, when this income is spent in communities, jobs are created. The authors discuss possible local strategies to capture cash transfers, including successful examples of development based on cash transfers. Formation of local capital pools with cash transfers and nationwide marketing strategies are suggested as possible options.

501.   Taff, Steven J., Glen C. Pulver, and Sydney D. Staniforth. *Are Small Community Banks Prepared to Make*

Complex Business Loans? R3263. Madison, Wisc.: University of Wisconsin, College of Agriculture Research Division, 1984. 14 pp.

Examines how prepared rural banks are to meet the business development needs of their communities, and determines the characteristics of the banks best prepared to meet those needs. The research was based on the premise that the extent to which local banks are able and willing to make complex loans is indicated by the size and complexity of the business investments they have handled previously. The authors believe that the greater a bank's experience in arranging large, complex business-loan packages, the better it will be prepared to do so in the future.

502. U.S. Department of Agriculture. *Rural Resources Guide: A Directory of Public and Private Assistance for Small Communities*. Washington, D.C.: USDA, Office of Rural Development Policy, Government Printing Office, 1984. 576 pp. (Doc. A102.8: R88)

Catalogs about 440 sources of national-level, public and private, technical and financial resource assistance in an effort to aid local governments and community leaders in identifying and locating sources of aid for rural growth and development.

503. Walzer, Norman, and David R. Chicoine, eds. *Financing Economic Development in the 1980s: Issues and Trends*. New York: Praeger Publishers, 1986. 233 pp.

Assembles current information on local economic development topics. Twelve chapters address a variety of development issues including the effect of business climate on employment growth, attracting high-technology industry, the state role in economic development, and the impact of federal fiscal and trade policies on economic development in the Midwest.

Contains items 344, 425, 453, 459, 492.

504. Williams, Gerry H. *The Impact of Conditions in the Municipal Bond Market on Community Services and Facilities: A Synthesis and Annotated Bibliography*. Mississippi State, Miss.: Southern Rural Development Center, 1982. 80 pp.

Discusses factors responsible for the significant increase in the cost of public debt, the future of the municipal bond market under existing conditions, and ways to facilitate access of localities to the municipal market. Williams then annotates relevant literature.

Planning and Assessment

505. American Economic Development Council. *Computer Applications in Economic Development: A Report to the Profession.* Schiller Park, Ill., circa 1987.
    Provides an overview of the experience of various economic developers attempting to use computers. The report examines problems economic development organizations have with computerizing, training, and trends in computerizing. Some case studies are examined.

506. Anderson, Randall S., Jay A. Leitch, and Cliff R. Fegert. *Guidelines for Economic Evaluation of Public Sector Water Resource Projects.* Agr. Econ. Rpt. 201. Fargo, N.Dak.: North Dakota Agr. Exp. Sta., Dept. Agr. Econ., 1985. 63 pp.
    Presents guidelines for the application of economic evaluation procedures in project analysis of public sector water development in North Dakota. A brief history of North Dakota water development and two case studies are included.

507. Arcelus, Francisco J. "An Extension of Shift-Share Analysis." *Growth and Change* 15, no. 1 (1984): 3-8.
    Discusses shift-share analysis, a technique that has been used extensively in regional economics to study the components of regional growth. The purpose of this paper is threefold: (1) to introduce a new component, the regional growth effect, into the traditional shift-share formulation, intended to measure the effect of the growth of a given region on the industries in its midst; (2) to bring into sharper focus the issue of differences in industry mixes among regions; and (3) to show and discuss the implications of the relationship of the revised shift-share model with the location quotient and economic base models.

508. Aronson, Nancy R., Glen C. Pulver, and Rueben C. Buse. *The Influence of Community Characteristics on the Level of Retail Trade.* Madison, Wisc.: University of Wisconsin, Dept. Agr. Econ., 1987. 30 pp.
    Analyzes those factors that influence the level of retail sales in small and medium-size communities in Wisconsin. The authors attempt to identify which community characteristics and initiatives affect the performance of the local retail trade sector.

509. Baker, Harold R.   "Rural Communities in the West:
     Keeping the Towns Viable."   *Agrologist* 10, no. 4 (Fall
     1981): 12-18.
     Examines some of the factors affecting rural town
     survivability.   Baker believes future viability depends
     largely on two factors: the quality of nearby natural
     resources and the will of residents to survive.

510. Bendavid-Val, Avrom.   *Regional and Local Economic
     Analysis for Practitioners*.   New York: Praeger
     Publishers, 1983.   191 pp.
     Written for a broad body of practitioners of local and
     regional development.   Part 1 reviews basic economic
     concepts behind the methods of regional analysis.   Part
     2 presents methods of analysis: basic regional statis-
     tical compendium, income measures, linkages, industrial-
     composition analysis, economic base analysis, and input-
     output analysis.   Part 3 contains information about the
     planning contexts in which the methods might be used.

511. Berry, Brian J.L.   *Strategies, Models, and Economic
     Theories of Development in Rural Regions*.   Agr. Econ.
     Rpt. No. 127.   Washington, D.C.: USDA, Economic
     Research Service, Government Printing Office, 1967.
     43 pp.   (Doc. A93.28: 127)
     Presents research approaches to different problem
     areas of rural poverty and economic development.
     Discussed are theories of regional growth (trade,
     location, and export theories), growth forecasting
     (shift-share, economic base, input-output analysis, and
     econometric and simulation models), developmental
     programming (spatial programming and activity analysis),
     determining a proper development region, and policies
     and strategies.

512. Blakely, Edward J., and Ted K. Bradshaw.   "New Roles for
     Community Developers in Rural Growth Communities."
     Journal of the Community Development Society 13, no. 2
     (1982): 101-20.
     Points out that community development in rural areas
     has long addressed the problem of declining communities,
     depressed economies, and unorganized populations.   The
     recent growth of rural communities and economies will
     drastically alter the role that community developers
     play.   Based on the survey responses of 533 new migrants
     to five different types of California rural communities,
     data are presented that illustrate the new types of
     issues, which community developers will need to address.

It is argued that the major role of community developers
will be to coordinate and facilitate organizations in
rural areas rather than to provide assistance to
individuals.

513. Brady, Raymond J., and Chin Ming Yang. "The Design and
      Implementation of a Regional Economic-Demographic
      Simulation Model." *Annals of Regional Science* 17, no.
      3 (1983): 1-22.
      Presents the results of a modeling design effort to
      link a hybrid regional input-output model to demo-
      graphic, labor force, and energy models for use in
      planning in the San Francisco Bay region. Extensive use
      of system feedback is a major component of this research
      effort. Summary results of the model outputs are
      presented in this paper.

514. Brucker, Sharon M., Steven E. Hastings, and William R.
      Latham, III. "Regional Input-Output Analysis: A
      Comparison of Five 'Ready-Made' Model Systems." *The
      Review of Regional Studies* 17, no. 2 (1987): 1-16.
      Discusses the evolution of regional input-output (I-0)
      modeling and compares alternative systems for developing
      nonsurvey I-0 models for small regions. Evaluation
      criteria include monetary cost, time cost, data and
      computer requirements, outputs provided, and flexi-
      bility.

515. Butler, Lorna Michael, and Robert O. Coppedge. *A
      Training Model: A Regional Approach to Changing
      Economic Conditions*. WREP 94. Corvallis, Ore.:
      Oregon State University, Western Rural Development
      Center, 1986. 11 pp.
      Describes the Hard Times regional training model that
      was implemented by the Western Rural Development Center
      in 1983-1984. This institutional partnership provided
      training to local citizens so they, in turn, could help
      their own communities cope with the consequences of
      economic decline.

516. Carter, K.A. "Inadequacies of the Traditional Labor
      Force Framework for Rural Areas: A Labor Utilization
      Framework Applied to Survey Data." *Rural Sociology*
      47, no. 3 (1982): 459-74.
      Examines the measurement and conceptual problems of
      the traditional labor force framework as well as the
      inaccuracy of official labor force estimates for
      nonmetropolitan counties. Survey data from three

nonmetropolitan counties are used in the application of
a labor utilization framework. The labor utilization
framework is viewed as a more meaningful approach to
rural labor force analysis than the traditional labor
force approach.

517. Center for Rural Manpower and Public Affairs. *Manpower
    Planning for Jobs in Rural America.* East Lansing,
    Mich.: Michigan State University, 1973. 222 pp.
    Overviews manpower planning and economic development,
    discusses the implications of the Rural Development Act
    of 1972, reviews the experience of the Economic Develop-
    ment Administration and the Cooperative Area Manpower
    Planning System in manpower planning and economic
    development in rural areas, and relates experiences from
    experimental Rural Manpower Delivery Systems.

518. Coon, Randal C., F. Larry Leistritz, Thor A. Hertsgaard,
    and Arlen G. Leholm. *The North Dakota Input-Output
    Model: A Tool for Analyzing Economic Linkages.* Ag.
    Econ. Rpt. No. 187. Fargo, N. Dak.: North Dakota
    State University, Agr. Exp. Sta., 1985. 54 pp.
    Explains the principles of input-output (I-O) analy-
    sis, describes the structure of the North Dakota I-O
    model, and explains how to interpret the results that
    may appear in a feasibility or economic contribution
    study.

519. Coppedge, Robert O. *Organizing a Small-Town Development
    Corporation.* Circular 491. Las Cruces, N.Mex.: New
    Mexico State University, Cooperative Extension
    Service, 1980. 8 pp.
    Recommends forming a local development corporation in
    small towns, then briefly overviews their role and
    advantages to the community. Steps to organizing a
    corporation, deciding on its profit or nonprofit status,
    obtaining operating funds, obtaining certification, and
    preparing bylaws are outlined.

520. Costello, Anthony J. "The Charrette Process: University-
    Based Design Teams Serve Indiana's Small Towns."
    Small Town 17, no. 6 (May-June 1987): 18-25.
    Describes the Community-Based Projects (CBP) program
    in the College of Architecture and Planning at Ball
    State University in Indiana. The program provides
    students with practical experience in urban planning and
    design, citizen participation methods, and neighborhood
    revitalization. The program provides the public and

private sectors with educational programs to improve
participation in the decision-making process of community planning, revitalization, and development.

521. Costello, Anthony J. "Taking the Basic Steps to
      Facilitate Downtown Revitalization." *Small Town* 17,
      no. 6 (May-June 1987): 14-17.
      Focuses on aspects of the initial phase of the
      downtown revitalization process--identifying the people
      who constitute the downtown area and composing a
      physical and economic profile of the area.

522. Crush, Teresa. "Thermopolis, Wyoming: Developing a
      Comprehensive Downtown Plan." *Small Town* 16, no. 2
      (September-October 1985): 16-21.
      Describes the four-part downtown revitalization
      program developed by the Main Street Center of the
      National Trust for Historic Preservation. The community
      attained the status of having the downtown area desig-
      nated as a historic district in the National Register of
      Historic Places. The community renovated storefronts
      and established annual promotions.

523. Cummings, Ronald G., Thomas A. Grigalunas, and Edmond E.
      Seay. "A Theoretical Framework For Rural Community
      Development." *Canadian Journal of Agricultural
      Economics* 22, no. 1 (1974): 58-64.
      Outlines a programming framework that allows one to
      confront directly the issues involved in evaluating (as
      opposed to resolving) alternative strategies for rural
      community development. The model is designed to focus
      on the allocation of the community's limited resources
      among development activities, where the community's
      resources are specified within a qualitative, as well as
      a quantitative, context.

524. Debertin, D.L., and G. L. Bradford. "Conceptualizing
      and Quantifying Factors Influencing Growth and
      Development of Rural Economies." *The Annals of
      Regional Science* 10, no. 1 (1976): 29-40.
      Develops a paradigm of relationships influencing the
      growth and development of rural economies. Causal
      relationships depicted in the paradigm are used as the
      basis for delineating a mathematical model that forms
      the foundation of an empirical analysis of forces
      influencing the growth and development of rural com-
      munities in Indiana. Alternative model estimation

techniques are discussed, and empirical findings provide quantitative estimates of relative weights on forces influencing growth and development.

525. Debertin, David L., and John M. Huie. "Projecting Economic Activity Within Towns and Cities." *Journal of Community Development Society* 6, no. 1 (1975): 123-34.
Estimates an econometric model designed to project economic activity in small and moderate-sized towns. Measures of economic activity used in the analysis are population, income, retail sales, and employment. Sample projections are provided for two Indiana towns.

526. Diamond, Joseph E., and Daniel A. Lass. "Application of an Economic Base Model for Community Planning: The Case of Killingly, Connecticut." *Northeastern Agricultural Economics Council Journal* 9, no. 2 (1980): 75-79.
Attempts to determine the sources of basic (export) activity in the town of Killingly, Connecticut, and the surrounding trade area and to calculate a basic employment multiplier for the area. The multiplier is then used to analyze the economic impacts that would be associated with industrial development in Killingly.

527. Dunn, Douglas, and Douglas C. Cox. *Small Town Strategy: Socioeconomic Indicators for Small Towns*. WREP 58. Corvallis, Ore.: Oregon State University, Western Rural Development Center, 1982, 11 pp.
Offers community leaders specific guidelines for setting up a local data collection system. Included are examples from the community of Willcox, Arizona. The data collection system outlined can provide accurate, up-to-date estimates of population, family income, and gross sales within a town's trade area. This local data system is based on four locally available indicators: (1) electric hook-ups to estimate present population, (2) school enrollment to project population trends, (3) sales tax collections to assess present economic activity, and (4) postal delivery service and postal receipts to provide a further estimate of population and economic activity in the community.

528. Edwards, Clark, and Robert Coltrane. "Areal Delineations for Rural Economic Development Research." *Agricultural Economics Research* 24, no. 3 (July 1972): 67-76.

     Shows that estimates of statistical parameters vary
     for alternative geographic aggregations and for alterna-
     tive delineations at a given level of aggregation, and
     that estimates of statistical parameters for alternative
     delineations vary as the level of structural disaggrega-
     tion of variables used in the analysis is varied.

529. Edwards, Clark. "Modeling Rural Growth." *American
     Journal of Agricultural Economics* 61, no. 5 (1979):
     967-72.
     Addresses three obstacles to modeling rural growth:
     models, data, and theory. Some of the obstacles are
     inherent in the way researchers approach the modeling
     process, some are attributed to limitations of available
     data, and others stem from failure to incorporate
     relevant theory.

530. Erickson, Donald B., and George D. Johnson. "Short-Run
     Determinants of Small Community Development." *Journal
     of Community Development Society* 2, no. 1 (1971): 39-
     47.
     Uses factor analysis methods to develop a procedure
     whereby researchers can use a number of variables for
     communities to rank them with the other communities in
     an area. Kansas communities were used for this study.

531. Eskelinen, Heikki. "Findings on Input-Output in a Small
     Area Context." *Annals of Regional Science* 17, no. 1
     (1983): 40-55.
     Compares two input-output (I-O) studies made at an
     interval of five years for a small regional economy in
     eastern Finland. Special attention is directed to the
     stability and influence of the most important coeffi-
     cients, which are identified on the basis of size and a
     special index. The conclusions derived accentuate the
     necessity of regional primary data in I-O accounts on
     the one hand, and the significance of random factors
     relating to the shifts of regional coefficients and
     their correspondence to the national ones are concerned
     on the other.

532. Fitzgerald, Joan, and Peter B. Meyer. "Recognizing
     Constraints to Local Economic Development." *Journal
     of the Community Development Society* 17, no. 2 (1986):
     115-26.
     Discusses the constraints on local economic develop-
     ment associated with increased concentration of capital,
     drawing on Kaufman's distinction between development *in*

the community and development of the community. The
likelihood of successfully employing "import substitution" and other localization strategies without con-
fronting issues of nonlocal control of the investment
process is also examined. Two options for responding to
capital constraints are discussed: (1) attempts to
restore the conditions for nonlocal private capital
accumulation in the community, and (2) attempts to
create alternative local investment institutions.

533. Fox, W.F., J.M. Stam, W.M. Godsey, and S.D. Brown.
*Economies of Size in Local Government: An Annotated
Bibliography.* Rural Development Research Report.
Washington, D.C.: USDA, Dept. Agriculture, Economics,
Statistics, and Cooperatives Service, April 1979. 74
pp.
Contains annotations for 133 papers, reports, and
books, which test for size or scale economies in
producing local government goods and services. Size
economies refer to the set of phenomena that cause
average costs of providing a good or service to decline
with increasing size of the government unit. This deals
solely with the supply side costs of providing services
and therefore excludes research on such topics as
expenditure determinants of local governments and
optimal city size. Research applying to size economies
results is generally omitted. An appendix lists some
research on these omitted topics.

534. Fujii, Edwin T., and James Mak. "The Impact of Alternative Regional Development Strategies on Crime Rates:
Tourism vs. Agriculture in Hawaii." *The Annals of
Regional Science* 13, no. 3 (1979): 42-56.
Examines the hypothesis that an alteration in the
composition of economic activity in the form of a
displacement of agriculture by resort development will
increase crime. Authors use a cross-sectional analysis
of the determinants of crime rates on the island of Oahu
in 1975 and a parallel time series analysis for Hawaii
from 1961 to 1975.

535. Gault, George H., and Robert O. Coppedge. *Small Town
Strategy: Community Evaluation for Economic Development.* WREP 59. Corvallis, Ore.: Oregon State
University, Western Rural Development Center, 1982.
10 pp.
Provides some guidelines for evaluating a community's
potential for different types of economic development.

536. Georgia Institute of Technology. *Evaluating Economic
      Development Programs: A Methodology Handbook.*
      Atlanta: Economic Development Laboratory, Engineering
      Experiment Station, Georgia Institute of Technology,
      1982. 152 pp.
      Offers guidance on evaluating economic development
      programs and organizations, the development process, the
      economic inventory of an area, job-location impacts,
      service impacts of infrastructure investment, and sudden
      economic dislocations.

537. Gittinger, J. Price. *Economic Analysis of Agricultural
      Projects.* Baltimore, Md.: Johns Hopkins University
      Press, 1982. 505 pp.
      Provides practitioners of agricultural investments in
      developing countries with analytical tools to estimate
      the income-generating potential of proposed projects.
      Gittinger discusses the project concept, identifying
      costs and benefits, analyzing processing industries,
      determining economic values, and measuring the project's
      worth.

538. Gordon, John, and David Darling. "Measuring Economic
      Growth in Rural Communities: The Shift-Share Ap-
      proach." *Southern Journal of Agricultural Economics*
      (December 1976): 73-78.
      Identifies changes that have taken place in the
      industrial composition of the local economy relative to
      a reference area or standard of comparison (nation,
      state, or region); explains differences in rates of
      growth; and identifies industries in which the study
      area has had a comparative advantage. Four Indiana
      counties were studied.

539. Gordon, John, and David Mulkey. "Income Multipliers for
      Community Impact Analyses--What Size is Reasonable?"
      Journal of Community Development Society 9, no. 1
      (1978): 85-93.
      Indicates that a personal income multiplier is
      extremely useful in community impact analyses. The
      multipliers used in impact studies are often derived
      with shortcut techniques and presented with little
      explanation of how they were constructed. To improve
      the ability of community development practitioners to
      evaluate economic impact statements and to estimate
      multipliers, insight is needed into the question of
      reasonable income-multiplier size. This article
      demonstrates that community personal income multipliers

are likely to be larger than 1.05 and less than 2.50.
The multiplier for a small- to medium-size community is
more likely to be within the range of 1.10 to 1.50.

540. Gould, Brian W. "The Impacts of Prairie Branch Line
      Rehabilitation: An Application of Interregional Input-
      Output Analysis." *Canadian Journal of Agricultural
      Economics* 34, no. 3 (1986): 313-30.
      Develops an interregional input-output model (PRAIRIO)
      of Canada. This model represents an application of the
      rectangular accounting system within a multiregional
      impact analysis. The development of such a model is
      important from a public policy perspective in that
      input-output analyses are often used as a part of an
      overall program evaluation or benefit cost analysis.

541. Guedry, Leo J., and David W. Smith. "Impact of Industry
      in Rural Economies." *Southern Journal of Agricultural
      Economics* 12, no. 2 (1980): 19-24.
      Presents a specification of an input-output model that
      will permit identification of distribution impacts
      associated with industry (or any other sector), and
      describes an empirical application of the model to the
      industrial sector of a small rural economy.

542. Hackbart, Merlin M., and Donald A. Anderson. "On
      Measuring Economic Diversification." *Land Economics*
      51 (November 1975): 374-78.
      Considers a method for measuring economic diversifica-
      tion as applied at state and regional levels in Wyoming.
      The method is the Shannon entropy function applied to
      sectorial employment shares.

543. Hamilton, Joel R., and Chaipant Pongtanakorn. "The
      Economic Impact of Irrigation Development in Idaho: An
      Application of Marginal Input-Output Methods." *Annals
      of Regional Science* 17, no. 2 (1983): 60-70.
      Estimates impacts of expanded irrigation in Idaho
      using marginal input-output. This makes it possible to
      account for changes in input use from the average input
      mix of existing sectors. Particular attention is given
      to the effect of new, energy-intensive irrigation on the
      overall demand for electricity, and on limited low-cost
      hydroelectric sources in particular.

544. Harris, Thomas R., and James C. Bezdek. *Fuzzy Cluster-
      ing for Regional Typology: A Nevada Example*. Reno,

Nev.: University of Nevada, Div. Agr. Econ. 1987.   16 pp.

Uses fuzzy cluster analysis to develop a typology of Nevada counties. Clustering using fuzzy sets provides membership values for each Nevada county that can be used to assess the extent to which each county belongs to each (fuzzy) partitioning subclass. Information from the fuzzy partitions yields a means for a posteriori evaluation of clusters, which can subsequently be used for specific and well-targeted economic development and diversification strategies.

545.   Harris, Thomas R. *Commercial Sector Development in Rural Communities: Trade Area Analysis.* WREP 90. Corvallis, Ore.: Oregon State University, Western Rural Development Center, 1985. 4 pp.

Points out that a comprehensive development strategy should not only encourage the attraction of export industries but also emphasize developing the community's commercial sector. Analytical tools for trade area analysis are discussed, and two specific measures (trade area capture and pull factor) are calculated.

546.   Henry, Mark S., Arlen Leholm, Glenn Schaible, and James Haskins. "A Semi-Survey Approach to Building Regional Input-Output Models: An Application to Western North Dakota." *North Central Journal of Agricultural Economics* 2, no. 1 (1980): 17-24.

Describes an input-output data collection methodology that combines primary and secondary data sources. This method's strong points are a uniform data base between sectors, a relatively low cost compared to gathering primary data, and an ability to incorporate data on new or expanding firms in a timely and inexpensive manner.

547.   Hirschl, Thomas A., and Gene F. Summers. "Cash Transfers and the Export Base of Small Communities." *Rural Sociology* 47, no. 2 (1982): 295-316.

Proposes an export base model of local employment growth where one of the "export" sectors is cash transfer payments to individuals. The basic sectors considered are agriculture, manufacturing, intergovernmental transfers, and cash transfers to individuals. The model is tested with a sample of U.S. counties using data from secondary sources. Cash transfers are found to have strong positive effects on local nonbasic employment growth. Manufacturing and agriculture were also found to have significant effects.

Also in the model are ecological qualities, such as
industrial diversity and urbanization of the local
community. The findings and hypotheses are discussed in
relation to the population turnaround of nonmetropolitan
communities, the growth of social welfare payments, the
economic significance of cash transfers to local
communities, and the Keynesian macro approach to
economic growth.

548. Honadle, B.W. *Capacity-Building (Management Improve-
      ment) for Local Governments: An Annotated Bibliog-
      raphy.* Rural Development Research Report 28.
      Washington, D.C.: USDA, Economics and Statistics
      Service, March 1981. 78 pp.
      Contains 162 annotations on the above topic, provides
an implicit and explicit definition of the terms
capacity and *capacity-building,* and determines the type
of capacity to which each publication refers.

549. Hordo, R.J., and J.A. MacMillan. "An Assessment of FRED
      Plan Management in the Interlake Region of Manitoba."
      Canadian Journal of Agricultural Economics 24, no. 1
      (1976): 33-48.
      Describes a management model designed for a rural
development plan in Manitoba. Issues include goal
setting, control, innovation, and intelligence. The
framework emphasizes the need to explicitly consider
communication flows between public managers and plan
clientele (local groups and individuals who are to
benefit from the plan).

550. Howe, Charles W. "On the Theory of Optimal Regional
      Development Based on an Exhaustible Resource." *Growth
      and Change* 18, no. 2 (1987): 53-68.
      Considers the effect of combining the optimization of
resource exploitation with optimization of population
growth and infrastructure investment. A model incor-
porating these dimensions of regional growth is analyzed
using control theory to characterize the optimal time
paths of the resource-related investment, resource use,
and infrastructure investment. An example of nonrenew-
able groundwater use in the Colorado High Plains region
is analyzed to show the shortcomings of existing
regulatory schemes.

551. Hua, Chang-i, and Frank Porell. "A Critical Review of
      the Development of the Gravity Model." *International
      Regional Science Review* 4, no. 2 (1979): 97-126.

Analyzes and criticizes recent work on gravity models
with respect to form, structure, derivation, and
theoretical and methodological grounds. The evolution
of the model is summarized, and a general form is
defined. The models are compared with regard to certain
structural properties--biproportionality, scale,
endogeny, consistency, and spatial interaction. The
various macro and micro approaches to deriving or
interpreting gravity models are reviewed. Problems and
limitations of each approach are noted, and their basic
theoretical foundations are criticized. Finally, the
general trend of gravity model development is discussed.

552. Hushak, L.J., G.W. Morse, and A. Osman. "Income and
     Fiscal Impact Analysis of Manufacturing Plants in
     Rural Southeastern Ohio." *North Central Journal of
     Agricultural Economics* 3, no. 2 (1981): 139-47.
     Estimates the net income and fiscal impacts generated
     by manufacturing plants on local, county, and regional
     communities in southeastern Ohio. Use of incremental
     income instead of consumption to measure primary
     benefits results in an increase in estimated net
     benefits. Increases progress from local to county and
     from county to regional levels.

553. Hushak, Leroy J., and Agyapong B. Gyekye. "The Rela-
     tionship Between Selected Economic and Demographic
     Measures and Employment/Specialization." *North
     Central Journal of Agricultural Economics* 6, no. 2
     (1984): 48-58.
     Examines whether counties can be classified into a
     usefully small number of prototype categories by
     classifying all counties in the North Central region
     into six prototypes on the basis of sectoral employment
     distributions in 1970. Although the discriminant model
     is statistically significant, county employment dis-
     tributions appear to be too complex for classification
     into a small number of prototypes.

554. Hustedde, Ron, Ron Shaffer, and Glen Pulver. *Community
     Economic Analysis*. Ames, Iowa: North Central Regional
     Center for Rural Development, Iowa State University,
     1984. 84 pp.
     Presents some community economic analysis tools useful
     in determining multipliers, assessing the size and shape
     of a community's trade area, measuring the efficiency of
     local firms, and keeping local dollars in the community.

555. Indiana State Planning Services Agency. *Community Revitalization Analysis: Methodology and Results*. Indianapolis, Ind., 1980. 92 pp.
   Reports the results of a project (1) to develop quantitative measures for ranking the economic condition of 551 communities in Indiana and (2) to identify communities in need of revitalization funds. Five factors were used in the analysis: population, personal income, housing, property assessed valuation, and employment.

556. International City Management Association. *Local Economic Development: A Strategic Approach*. Washington, D.C., 1984. 80 pp.
   Is a training package consisting of a handbook, a user's guide, and a set of sample survey instruments and data collection sheets. It discusses how megatrends affect local communities, examines the roles of public and private sectors, examines key local government actions to promote economic growth, identifies factors in the local climate that influence economic growth, and emphasizes the importance of making comparisons with other communities on these factors (quality of life, labor, land, capital, and market characteristics).

557. Isserman, Andrew M. "Estimating Export Activity in a Regional Economy: A Theoretical and Empirical Analysis of Alternative Methods." *International Regional Science Review* 5, no. 2, (1980): 155-84.
   Examines the theoretical rationales of four methods of estimating exports widely used in regional analysis, particularly the economic base model. An interpretation of the minimum requirement method is offered, which solves the nonimportation problem. The difference between the minimum requirement and location quotient estimates is proven not to be an estimate of imports as is widely believed, and a relatively new econometric method is shown to overestimate exports. Estimates of exports are calculated for 101 metropolitan areas in the United States. The results suggest that the choice of estimation method may affect the results of subsequent analyses.

558. Johns, P.M., and P.M.K. Leat. "The Application of Modified GRIT Input-Output Procedures To Rural Development Analysis in the Grampian Region." *Journal of Agricultural Economics* 38, no. 2 (1987): 243-56.

Points out that, while the production of regional input-output matrices by survey methods is extremely expensive, an alternative method is to adjust mechanistically a national input-output table by an employment-based location quotient procedure. The authors discuss some important conceptual issues related to this methodology and also present the main findings of a model for the Grampian region of Scotland. The model's implications for regional and rural development are assessed by multiplier analysis.

559. Johnson, Thomas G. "A Dynamic Input-Output Model for Small Regions." *The Review of Regional Studies* 16, no. 1 (1986): 14-23.
Develops a conceptual foundation for temporal input-output, reviews the experiences in the area, and looks at its potential, particularly for small-region modeling. Finally, a particular dynamic input-output model is described and examined in light of this conceptual foundation.

560. Jordan, Jeffrey L., and Rusty Brooks. "IO/EAM: An Input-Output Economic Assessment Model." *Southern Journal of Agricultural Economics* 16, no. 2 (1984): 145-49.
Describes a microcomputer software package developed at the University of Georgia to estimate the impact of changes in county economies on an industry-by-industry basis and to account for the interdependencies among these industries.

561. Katz, Joseph L., and Roger L. Burford. "Shortcut Formulas for Output, Income and Employment Multipliers." *Annals of Regional Science* 19, no. 2 (1985): 61-76.
Points out that, although input-output models provide a method to measure the output, income, and employment impacts of an industry sector on its regional economy, the extensive data requirements make the construction of an accurate survey-based input-output model extremely expensive. Using the "random matrix approach," the authors derive and empirically test shortcut formulas for output, income, and employment impacts that closely approximate the actual effects.

562. Kau, James B., and C.F. Sirmans. "The Functional Form of the Gravity Model." *International Regional Science Review* 4, no. 2 (1979): 127-36.

States that gravity models have been used extensively
in regional planning and transportation studies in order
to examine spatial interaction, but these models have
been criticized because their precise functional form is
difficult to determine empirically. An application of a
maximum likelihood method, developed by Box and Cox, is
presented that allows an investigator to choose the most
appropriate functional form from a general class of
alternatives. This method, which imposes no additional
information requirements, is applied to 1970 data on 489
trip flows among approximately 700 different travel
nodes in Georgia. The log-linear functional form for
the gravity model performs best in this context.

563. Khan, M. Shahbaz, and George I. Treyz. "A Community
     Economic Forecasting and Simulation System: Descrip-
     tion of a Satellite Model." *Growth and Change* 18, no.
     2 (1987): 1-14.
     Deals with the problem of modeling subcounty areas
     that are so small that county-level forecasts cannot be
     used for policy purposes. Starting from a simple
     specification that relates demand for local goods and
     services to local and nonlocal income, the authors
     develop a system of equations that can be used as a
     satellite to a county model to forecast impacts of
     economic events at the town level. An example of an
     application is provided by simulating impacts of 500 new
     manufacturing jobs in a town.

564. Kiser, Janet. "County Survey Valuable Tool in Rural
     Development." *Rural Development Perspectives* 3, no. 3
     (June 1987): 34-38.
     Relates the experiences of officials of Pend Oreille
     County, Washington, who surveyed the county in response
     to concern over a proposed new pulp mill. The survey
     proved useful in later helping the county obtain new
     grants to improve roads and sewers and to enhance the
     county's health care system.

565. Krider, Charles E., and Douglas A. Houston. "Economic
     Prospects for Rural Communities." *Kansas Policy
     Choices: Report of the Special Commission on a Public
     Agenda for Kansas.* (item 640), pp. 49-74.
     Examines the economic situation of rural communities
     in Kansas and prospects for the future. The focus is
     upon current economic and demographic trends and what
     these imply for the ability of rural communities to
     adapt to changing conditions. Certain essential

services provided to rural Kansas (for example, transportation and public utilities) are then analyzed.
Finally, the policy choices posed by these analyses are
presented with emphasis on stimulating economic development in rural communities.

566. Kuehn, J.A., M. Fessehaye, C. Braschler, and B. McGill.
     *Analyzing the Feasibility of Domestic Rural Water
     Supplies in Missouri with Emphasis on the Ozarks
     Region.* Columbia: University of Missouri, January
     1980. 56 pp.
     Presents a method by which community leaders and
     decision makers can perform a preliminary feasibility
     study of proposed rural and small town domestic water
     systems. Specific objectives include (1) estimating
     construction cost items for water supply systems, (2)
     estimating operating costs for different types of
     systems, (3) presenting engineering aspects needed for a
     preliminary feasibility study, (4) estimating water
     supply requirements, (5) calculating water rates needed
     to pay all costs, (6) applying the above analyses to a
     specific demonstration area, and (7) developing techni-
     ques that other community leaders and decision makers
     can use for analyzing proposed water supply systems.

567. Kuehn, John A., Michael H. Procter, and Curtis H.
     Braschler. "Comparisons of Multipliers from Input-
     Output and Economic Base Models." *Land Economics* 61,
     no. 2 (1985): 129-35.
     Compares multipliers from a nonsurvey, simply con-
     structed input-output model with those of a semisurvey,
     intensively developed model for the state of Missouri.
     The nonsurvey model is then used to estimate earnings
     multipliers for Missouri's nonmetropolitan counties, and
     the multipliers are compared with economic base multi-
     pliers for nonmetropolitan counties in a midwestern
     region.

568. Lassey, William R., and Nicholas P. Lovrich, Jr. "A
     Rural Development Model with Potential International
     Applications." *Journal of Rural Studies* 1, no. 3
     (1985): 267-77.
     Reports on a major project in rural planning and
     development that was initiated in the eastern counties
     of Washington State beginning in 1976. The purpose was
     to merge several previous models within a new conceptual
     framework incorporating collaboration among diverse
     organizations as a means of integrating development

activity. Institutions of higher education, state and federal agencies, regional secondary education organizations, a regional educational laboratory, counties, and local communities, among other units, were drawn together initially as members of the partnership.

569. Leuck, D.J. "An Econometric Model of Manufacturing Employment Growth in Rural Tennessee Counties from 1962 to 1976." *Southern Journal of Agricultural Economics* 11, no. 2 (1979): 63-67.
Describes a model that accounts for the effect of national economic trends on the level of total manufacturing employment in Tennessee and the influence of modifiable and nonmodifiable community characteristics on the distribution of total manufacturing employment among rural counties.

570. Lewis, Eugene, Russell Youmans, George Goldman, and Garnet Premer. *Economic Multipliers: Can a Rural Community Use Them?* WREP 24. Corvallis, Ore.: Oregon State University, Western Rural Development Center, 1979. 4 pp.
Explains the concept of the economic multiplier, shows how they are used in calculating impacts, and provides criteria for determining whether a given multiplier can be used in a specific situation. The discussion is directed to practitioners and especially to those concerned with small rural regions or local economies.

571. Long, Celeste, Mike Woods, and L.L. Jones. "Computer Model Helps Communities Gauge Effects of New Industry." *Rural Development Perspectives* 3, no. 3 (1987): 21-24.
Describes a computerized model used by rural planners in many Texas communities to analyze the benefits and costs associated with the establishment of new firms. The Industrial Impact Model is used to estimate the effects of a new development on a community's private and public sectors.

572. Luloff, A.E., and W. H. Chittenden. "Rural Industrialization: A Logit Anaylsis." *Rural Sociology* 49, no. 1 (1984): 67-88.
Examines the location of new manufacturing industries in 221 rural New Hampshire Minor Civil Divisions.

573. Lundeen, A.A., and L.L. Janssen. "Selected Impacts of a Large-Scale Rural Water System in South Dakota."

North Central Journal of Agricultural Economics 3, no.
2 (1981): 131-37.
Identifies potential impacts of a rural water system
on the public sector. Changes in demand for public
services and changes in the real property tax base were
the predominant effects. These impacts were estimated
and incorporated with policy variables to simulate the
effects of the development of a rural water system on
public sector expenditures and revenues. The model was
applied to a case study of the Brookings-Deuel Rural
Water System. In this case, for almost every government
entity, revenues were greater than expenditures.

574. McGranahan, D.A. "Local Growth and the Outside Contacts
      of Influentials: An Alternative Test of the 'Growth
      Machine' Hypothesis." *Rural Sociology* 49, no. 4
      (1984): 530-40.
      Builds from the premise that effective promotion
depends on experience and contacts with the larger
society to investigate relationships among the extralo-
cal participation of influentials, state and federal
program participation, and growth in manufacturing and
population during the 1970s in eighty-eight small
northwestern Wisconsin towns. The results are consistent with the model, although manufacturing and population growth did not occur in the same places in the
region.

575. McKean, J.R., W. Trock, and D.R. Senf. *An Interindustry
      Analysis of Three Front Range Foothills Communities:
      Estes Park, Gilpin County, and Woodland Park, Colo-
      rado.* Tech. Rpt. Fort Collins, Colo.: Colorado State
      University, Colorado Water Resources Research In-
      stitute, July 1982. 153 pp.
      Provides a description and analysis of three Front
Range foothills economies in eastern Colorado. The
intent of the researchers is to provide policymakers
with specific information contributing to Forest Service
decision-making and planning processes and to provide a
planning tool having the capability of analyzing a
number of alternative development scenarios in the study
regions.

576. MacMillan, J.A., and J.D. Graham. "Rural Development
      Planning: A Science?" *American Journal of Agricul-
      tural Economics* 60, no. 4 (1978): 945-49.
      Discusses testing rural development planning with
respect to (1) a proposed definition of research steps;

(2) a summary of research conducted for the evaluation of the rural development plans for the Interlake Region of Manitoba; (3) the applicability of the research steps for rural development planning in British Columbia; and (4) observations on rural development planning.

577. MacMillan, J.A., D.F. Kraft, and D. Ford. "Impacts of Agricultural Stabilization Programs on Development of Rural Communities." *Canadian Journal of Agricultural Economics* 24 (March 1976): 159-77.
Identifies mechanisms by which stabilization programs affect the development of rural communities, provides information concerning the likely pay-out and income distribution impacts of grain stabilization programs in the Prairie region, and describes the effects of stabilization on farm input purchases.

578. MacMillan, James A., Charles F. Framingham, and Fu-lai Tung. "A Proposed Simulation Method for Measuring Structural Change and Rural Development Program Impacts." *Canadian Journal of Agricultural Economics* 22, no. 1 (1974): 26-41.
Points out that a number of agricultural development programs have been designed in Canada to increase agricultural productivity and improve incomes of low-income farms in marginal agricultural areas. A dynamic regional model of agriculture with an explicit linkage between the development programs and the regional economy (including rural and urban dimensions) is proposed.

579. Malizia, Emil E. "Economic Development in Smaller Cities and Rural Areas." *American Planning Association* 52 (1986): 489-99.
Argues for an approach local leaders and professionals should use for economic development in smaller cities and rural areas. They should define economic development explicitly, using theory to articulate the public goals they want to pursue. They may locate the economic development function in public or private agencies, but they should use local development organizations--private entities created to achieve public economic development goals--to carry out economic development activities. Rural professionals should formulate a range of economic development strategies intended to achieve public goals and should establish priorities among them. For any rural area, unique strategies based on careful, unbiased

analysis and appropriate theory hold the most economic
development potential.

580. Mandelbau, Thomas B. *Sectoral Output Multipliers for
       Rural Counties: Lessons from Oregon's Input-Output
       Studies.* EC 1166. Corvallis, Ore.: Oregon State
       University Extension Service, 1984. 11 pp.
       Is designed both as an introduction to multipliers for
       the practitioner and as a guide to help them select the
       appropriate multiplier for a given application.

581. Marousek, Gerald, and Don Blayney. *Identifying Poten-
       tial Development in Rural Communities--A Statistical
       Approach.* Res. Bull. 111. Moscow: University of
       Idaho, September 1979. 12 pp.
       Has as its objectives to (1) identify and group Idaho
       communities according to common factors that can serve
       as proxies for measuring economic vitality, (2) apply
       the analysis to previously defined areas, and (3)
       examine economic change in the communities and areas
       identified.

582. Miernyk, William H. *Regional Analysis and Regional
       Policy.* Cambridge, Mass.: Oelgeschlager, Gunn, and
       Hain Publishers, 1982. 143 pp.
       Consists of three related parts. Part 1 includes two
       state-of-the-art essays. The first deals with inter-
       regional and multiregional input-output models, and the
       second is a review of the literature on regional and
       interregional econometric models. Part 2 consists of
       four short essays about the evaluation of regional
       development policy in the United States and evaluations
       of specific programs. The last part discusses some
       basic issues in regional economics.

583. Miller, Donald. "Project Location Analysis Using the
       Goals Achievement Method of Evaluation." *American
       Planning Association Journal* 46 (1980): 195-208.
       Describes how an analytical method was developed and
       applied in a Washington community to aid in selecting
       neighborhoods for rehabilitation loan assistance. Other
       locational problems involving multiple objectives can
       also be addressed using this evaluation procedure.

584. Moore, Craig L., and Marilyn Jacobsen. "Minimum
       Requirements and Regional Economics, 1980." *Economic
       Geography* 60, no. 3 (1984): 217-24.

Updates the use of empirical estimates made in 1974
using the minimum requirements technique to approximate
the percentage of the labor force expected to be
employed in each sector of a region's economy depending
on its population.

585. Mulligan, Gordon F. "Employment Multipliers and
      Functional Types of Communities: Effects of Public
      Transfer Payments." *Growth and Change* 18, no. 3
      (1987): 1-11.
      Identifies the difference between the traditional (or
average) base multiplier and the impact (or marginal)
base multiplier and demonstrates why a direct relationship should exist between the traditional base multiplier and the size of the community economy. The author
also demonstrates how solely employment-generated
estimates of the impact base multiplier tend to be
biased upward; that is, unless transfer payments are
specified in the ordinary-least-squares regression
equation, the impact of basic employment on nonbasic
employment tends to be somewhat exaggerated.

586. Mulligan, Gordon F., and Lay James Gibson. "A Note on
      Sectoral Multipliers in Small Communities." *Growth
      and Change* 15, no. 4 (1984): 3-7.
      Points out that, while sectoral multipliers have been
estimated in a variety of disaggregated economic base
studies, few of these multiplier models have been
actually calibrated at the community level. The authors
address this research deficiency by disclosing sectoral
multiplier estimates for communities with populations
between 1,000 and 15,000. These estimates were generated from an extensive primary data base that was
assembled between 1975 and 1982 in the U.S. Southwest.
This data base summarizes the employment and selling
characteristics of virtually every business establishment in a diverse group of communities.

587. Mulligan, Gordon F., and Lay James Gibson. "Regression
      Estimates of Economic Base Multipliers for Small
      Communities." *Economic Geography* 60 (1984): 225-37.
      Uses a comprehensive, cross-sectional data set to
calibrate the economic base model for small communities.
Four alternative methods are discussed and evaluated.
The analysis indicates that the base multiplier can be
accurately estimated if the total employment and public
transfer payments of a community are known.

588. *National Council for Urban Economic Development. Small*
      City Economic Development: Professional Development
      Program. Washington, D.C., 1984. 400 pp.
      Is a training manual to guide small city officials in
      comprehensive local economic development programs and
      activities, including using the Community Development
      Block Grant program. Topics include organizational
      options, community evaluation, financing, small business
      assistance programs, revitalizing commercial districts,
      and initiatives to retain and attract industries.

589. Nebraska Department of Economic Development. *Do It!:*
      The Nebraska Community Action Handbook. Lincoln,
      Nebr., n.d. 176 pp.
      Prepared as a guide to communities undertaking a
      comprehensive local economic development program. The
      looseleaf notebook contains sections on the development
      process, conducting community attitude surveys, for-
      mulating development goals and strategies, and locating
      public financial resources. Numerous sample worksheets,
      questionnaires, checklists, and press releases are
      included.

590. Nelson, J.R., and S.R. Gilbert. *User's Guide to a*
      Computer Program to Analyze Economic Feasibilities for
      Rural Mobile Home Park Developments. Stillwater,
      Okla.: Oklahoma State University, Agr. Exp. Sta.,
      August 1983. 20 pp.
      Describes a program to evaluate the economic feasi-
      bilities of mobile home park (MHP) developments in rural
      Oklahoma communities. The purpose of this user's manual
      is to explain the operating procedures of the MHP
      program.

591. Nelson, Marlys Knutson, and Lloyd D. Bender. *Choosing*
      Among Local Impact Models. Rural Dev. Res. Rpt. No.
      63. Washington, D.C.: USDA, Economic Research
      Service, November 1986. 33 pp.
      Summarizes the features, capabilities, and limitations
      of large-scale impact models and assesses the kinds of
      information produced and the differences in the techni-
      ques used in the estimation process. Sixteen models are
      evaluated according to (1) the number of estimates made,
      (2) the sequence in which estimates are made, (3)
      interrelationships among estimates in the model, and (4)
      the techniques used in the estimating process.

592. Pagoulatos, A., K. Mattas, and D.L. Debertin. "A
     Comparison of Some Alternatives to Input-Output
     Multipliers." *Land Economics* 62, no. 4 (November
     1986): 371-77.
     Makes empirical comparisons between estimates based on
     short-cut approaches and multipliers from a standard
     input-output model. Calculated internal indices of
     purchases and sales are contrasted with estimates from
     the matrix triangulation procedure.

593. Plaut, Thomas R. "An Econometric Model for Forecasting
     Regional Population Growth." *International Regional
     Science Review* 6, no. 1 (1981): 53-70.
     Estimates an econometric model for forecasting net
     migration and natural increase using time-series data
     for Texas. The model is simulated five years out-of-
     sample and found to be quite accurate in forecasting
     future population growth. It outperforms simpler
     prediction methods, thus indicating that explicit
     modeling of net migration and natural increase is
     superior to modeling only total population.

594. Powers, Ronald C., and Daryl J. Hobbs. "Changing
     Relationships Between Farm and Community." *The Farm
     and Food System in Transition: Emerging Policy Issues.*
     FS46. East Lansing, Mich.: Michigan State University,
     Cooperative Extension Service, 1985. 6 pp.
     Examines changes in relationships between agriculture
     and rural communities that have occurred since 1950 and
     discusses the implications of the changing relationship
     with respect to agricultural and rural development
     policy issues. The authors indicate that agriculture
     has become a less important part of the economic base of
     many communities and that increasingly the structure of
     farming is affected by the nature of the rest of the
     area economy.

595. Redwood, Anthony L., and Gary R. Albrecht. "The Kansas
     Economy." *Kansas Policy Choices: Report of the Special
     Commission on a Public Agenda for Kansas* (item 640),
     pp. 21-47.
     Assesses the Kansas economy and identifies policy
     choices now facing Kansas decision makers as they seek
     to position the state for the next century. The
     assessment was based on an analysis of the evolution,
     current status, and outlook of the state's economic and
     demographic environment. The authors conclude that the

economy is not well positioned to go forward strongly in
the next decade, so that restructuring the economic
sector for a more prosperous future constitutes a
primary challenge for Kansans in the years ahead.

596. Reid, J.N., T.F. Stinson, P.J. Sullivan, L.B. Perkinson,
     M.P. Clarke, and E. Whitehead. *Availability of
     Selected Public Facilities in Rural Communities:
     Preliminary Estimates*. ERS Staff Rpt. AGES 840113.
     Washington, D.C.: USDA, Economic Research Service,
     March 1984. 51 pp.
     Presents preliminary estimates for a selection of
     variables from the National Rural Commmunity Facilities
     Assessment Study, a nationwide sample survey of the
     availability and condition of essential public facili-
     ties in rural America. The variables were chosen to
     indicate the availability of facilities in rural
     America. Included in this report are data collected by
     survey for public water supply, fire protection, and
     local roads and bridges. Also included are national
     estimates for wastewater treatment, hospital, and
     nursing home facilities drawn from secondary data
     sources.

597. Rubin, Herbert J. "Local Economic Development Organiza-
     tions and the Activities of Small Cities in Encourag-
     ing Economic Growth." *Policy Studies Journal* 14, no.
     3 (1986): 363-88.
     Offers a speculative model describing the effects a
     local economic development organization has upon the
     number of activities to promote economic development
     attempted by small and middle-size municipalities. The
     model measures the incremental effect over and above
     that explained by background economic and social
     factors.

598. Schautz, Jane W. *The Self-Help Handbook*. Rensselaer-
     ville, N.Y.: Rensselaerville Institute, 1985. 199
     pp.
     Details a new program developed by the Rensselaerville
     Institute in conjunction with other agencies to focus on
     improving or creating water and wastewater systems in
     small rural communities. The book supplies a variety of
     techniques for making the best possible use of available
     local resources to cut project costs and make capital
     improvements within the reach of small towns.

599. Shahidsaless, Shahin, William Gillis, and Ron Shaffer.
"Community Characteristics and Employment Multipliers
in Nonmetropolitan Counties, 1950-1970." *Land
Economics* 59, no. 1 (1983): 84-93.
Presents results of a systematic examination of
community characteristics that condition the magnitude
of local multiplier impacts. The hypothesis tested is
that community economic growth or decline is a function
of the type of exogenous employment change and a vector
of community characteristics, including location and
population.

600. Smith, Christine. "Determining Economic Base--A Process
of Community Study." *Journal of the Community
Development Society* 15, no. 2 (1984): 73-85.
Examines a specific study aimed at determining the
economic base of a rural community. A general description of the concept of economic base and how it is
studied is provided. A case study of one community
study process is delineated by benchmark events. The
function of community development principles, such as
citizen involvement and organizational cooperation, is
described. The importance of outside technical assistance is pointed out as a perceived and actual need of
the group sponsoring the economic base study.

601. Smith, Eldon D., Brady J. Deaton, and David R. Kelch.
"Location Determinants of Manufacturing Industry in
Rural Areas." *Southern Journal of Agricultural
Economics* 10, no. 1 (1978): 23-32.
Presents a model for analyzing statistically the
industrial development potentials and investment risks
for local decisionmakers. Batie (item 350) discusses
the authors' method and theoretical specification of the
function used.

602. Stevens, Benjamin H., George I. Treyz, David J. Ehrlich,
and James R. Bower. "A New Technique for the Construction of Non-Survey Regional Input-Output Models."
International Regional Science Review 8, no. 3 (1983):
271-86.
Tests a technique for creating regional input-output
models based on national input-output technological
coefficients. The Regional Purchase Coefficient (RPC),
i.e., the proportion of regional demand fulfilled from
regional production, is based on substitution between
extra- and intraregional sources in response to relative
delivered costs. An RPC estimating equation is fitted

using state economic and interstate transportation data.
The RPCs for all sectors are estimated for use in
constructing 500-sector nonsurvey models for Washington
and West Virginia.

603. Taylor, Nick. "Social Assessment for Rural Develop-
      ment." *People and Planning* 38 (1986): 2-4.
      Illustrates recent applications of social impact
assessment techniques to several types of rural socioeconomic change, including diversification of traditional farming through irrigation and horticulture, land
development for pastoral farming, and investigations of
issues concerning the viability of services in small
rural towns.

604. Tennessee Valley Authority. *Redark Symposium on
      Economic Development Leadership--Symposium Workbook.*
      Knoxville, Tenn., 1986. 150 pp.
      Designed for small towns and rural areas in Oklahoma,
but is applicable to other states. Topics include the
role of community leaders, encouraging home-grown job
creation, surveying and assessing industry needs and
business operators, attracting new industry, and
preparing the community for economic development.

605. Thomas, Margaret G. *A Rural Economic Development
      Sourcebook: Selected Training and Technical Assistance
      Materials.* Kansas City, Mo.: Midwest Research
      Institute and Economic Development Administration,
      revised 1987. 100 pp. plus appendixes.
      Describes recent training and technical assistance
materials useful in preparing rural economic development
strategies. The work is intended for use by public
officials, community leaders, and rural development
practitioners. Major categories of source materials
include those dealing with planning and organizing,
economic development strategies, and tools and techniques.

606. U.S. Congress, House. *Rural Community Development Act
      and Rural Development Policy Act.* Hearings before the
      Subcommittee on Family Farms, Rural Development, and
      Special Studies. Washington, D.C.: Government
      Printing Office, 1978. 593 pp. (Doc. Y4.Ag8/1:
      R88/23)
      Presents statements regarding H.R. 9983, a bill to
establish a separate community development program for
units of general local government that have a population

of 20,000 or fewer and are located in nonmetropolitan areas, and regarding H.R. 10885, a bill to establish a council to assist in meeting the development needs of rural areas of the United States.

607. U.S. Department of Agriculture. *Rural Economic Develop-
      ment in the 1980's: Preparing For the Future.* ERS
      Staff Rpt. No. AGES 870724. Washington, D.C.: USDA,
      Economic Research Service, 1987. 410 pp.
      Reports that structural change in the economy is
      causing economic stress in rural America, in sharp
      contrast with the 1970s, when growth and economic
      vitality were the dominant rural themes. The papers in
      this volume provide up-to-date information on changes in
      the structure and performance of the rural economy and
      on alternative policies to facilitate the adjustment of
      displaced people and their communities.
      Contains items 302, 324, 337, 355, 623, 660.

608. Webb, S.H., G.A. Doeksen, and R. Carroll. *A Community
      Development Guide for a Transportation System for the
      Elderly.* Bulletin B-757. Stillwater, Okla.: Oklahoma
      Agr. Exp. Sta., Oklahoma State University, May 1981.
      26 pp.
      Provides cost and income information for various
      alternatives and a methodology for the estimation of a
      community's needs for a transportation system for the
      elderly. Planners should integrate local information in
      their alternatives so that each closely reflects the
      community's conditions and needs. The forms and data in
      this guide can be used to develop costs and revenue for
      a county system with multiple locations and routes.

609. Weber, Bruce A., and Shepard C. Buchanan. "The Impact
      of Population Growth on Residential Property Taxes."
      Western Journal of Agricultural Economics 5, no. 2
      (1980): 177-84.
      Uses cross-sectional data from Oregon to estimate a
      multivariate model of the effect of population on local
      fiscal behavior, assessed value of property, and average
      single-family home values. Results indicate that
      property tax levies are unit elastic with respect to
      population, that the assessed value of property in-
      creases less than proportionally with population, and
      that the average value of a single-family home increases
      with population.

610. Weber, Bruce A., Stephen M. Smith, Ronald C. Faas, and
      Gary W. Smith. *Understanding Your Local Economy:
      Economic Base Analysis and Local Development Strat-
      egies.* WRDC 29. Corvallis, Ore.: Oregon State
      University, Western Rural Development Center, 1986.
      11 pp.
      Explains the process of local employment and income
      generation, illustrates several simple techniques for
      estimating the local economic base, and suggests how
      information on economic structure can be used to help
      select more promising economic development strategies.

611. Weitz, J.A. *Getting Your Community Ready for Economic
      Development.* EC-581. Lafayette, Ind.: Purdue
      University, Cooperative Extension Service, April 1982.
      7 pp.
      Explains how volunteer citizen leaders in small, rural
      towns can examine and prepare themselves for economic
      development.

612. Weitz, J.A. *The Community Checklist: A Tool for
      Community Needs Identification.* EC-580. Lafayette,
      Ind.: Purdue University, Cooperative Extension
      Service, June 1982. 20 pp.
      Is designed to assist volunteer citizen leaders in
      small, rural towns to identify community needs and set
      priorities for community development.

613. Williams, D.G. *Economic Planning for Multicounty Rural
      Areas: Application of a Linear Programming Model in
      Northwest Arkansas.* Tech. Bull. 1653. Washington,
      D.C.: USDA, June 1981. 75 pp.
      States that using a linear programming economic
      development model can help regional planners influence
      the most desirable type of growth for rural areas.
      Optimal resource use, investment, and industry mix for
      manufacturing, services, government, and agriculture are
      reviewed for nine regional macroeconomic goals, with the
      tradeoffs evaluated for attaining one objective over
      another. Multiple regression analysis allows the most
      desirable industries to be identified by economic
      characteristics, such as capital/output and value
      added/labor, rather than by product type.

614. Williams, Daniel G. "Objective Function Tradeoff Curves
      in a Rural Economic Development, Activity Analysis
      Planning Model." *Annals of Regional Science* 15, no. 3
      (1981): 55-72.

Examines pairs of economic objectives for a multicounty planning region (e.g., maximize balance-of-trade surplus, maximize local employment) and derives tradeoff curves, which might prove useful to planners. Several objectives examined might be considered as capital-oriented (e.g., maximizing trade surplus). These objectives yield regional economic outcomes more similar to each other than to outcomes from labor-oriented objectives (e.g., maximizing local employment). The results suggest that conflicts may increase as regions become more open to trade and commuting; the need for compromise among differing local interests increases accordingly.

615. Williams, Daniel G. "Regional Development as Determined by Alternative Regional Goals." *Growth and Change* 14, no. 3 (1983): 23-37.
    Examines for a small, multicounty region the relationships among alternative regional growth goals and the differences in such characteristics as industry mix and increases in regional wage and gross regional product that these different growth goals imply. Three counties in northwestern Arkansas are studied.

616. Woods, M.D., G.A. Doeksen, and J.R. Nelson. "Community Economics: A Simulation Model for Rural Development Planners." *Southern Journal of Agricultural Economics* 15, no. 2 (1983): 71-77.
    Presents a simulation model for rural communities and summarizes its application for an Oklahoma community. Some variables projected annually include employment and income by sector, and population by age-sex cohort. Community service requirements, such as hospital bed-days, physician visits, water, sewer, fire protection, and solid waste are projected. Also, local community revenue is estimated.

617. Woods, Mike D., and Gerald A. Doeksen. "A Simulation Model for Community Development Planning." *Journal of the Community Development Society* 15, no. 2 (1984): 47-57.
    Presents a community-level simulation model, designed for planning and addressing the issues of community growth and change. The simulation model provides annual projections for community employment, income, and population. Community service requirements for water, sewer, solid waste, ambulance calls, physician visits,

hospital bed days, and fire calls are also projected.
Results of a model application are presented.

Policies and Issues

618. Allen, David N., and Victor Levine. *Nurturing Advanced
      Technology Enterprises: Emerging Issues in State and
      Local Economic Development Policy.* New York: Praeger
      Publishers, 1986. 268 pp.
      Examines the changing nature of the U.S. economy and
      governmental policies promoting economic development.
      Specifically, the book focuses on how public policy may
      affect the behavior of advanced-technology firms and how
      the behavior of these firms, in turn, may affect the
      nation's social and economic environment. The authors
      point out that public policy is a way of engineering
      change purposefully, and advanced technology is an
      important agent in that change.

619. Allen, Kevin, ed. *Balanced National Growth.* Lexington,
      Mass.: Lexington Books, 1979. 331 pp.
      Draws together papers on the European and Canadian
      experiences in regional economic incentive policy and
      applies it to U.S. policy options. The European
      countries are Great Britain, France, the Federal
      Republic of Germany, the Netherlands, and Italy.

  *   *The Annals of the American Academy of Political and
      Social Science.* Special Issue: *Deindustrialization:
      Restructuring the Economy.* Cited above as item 25.

620. Barsh, Russell Lawrence, and Jeffrey Gale. "U.S.
      Economic Development Policy--The Urban-Rural Dimen-
      sion." *Policy Studies Journal* 10, no. 2 (1981): 248-
      71.
      Reviews economic development in the U.S. context from
      the federal level. Appropriate intervention into free
      market processes is examined as to justifications and
      unit of analysis. Economic development policy history
      is reviewed and sociopolitical scenarios are introduced
      to explain patterns toward industrialization.

621. Behnke, Paul, and Christopher Bond. "Meeting Rural
      Needs: The Role of State and Local Governments." *The
      Rural Sociologist* 4, no. 5 (1984): 354-63.

Outlines some trends occurring throughout the member
countries of the Organization for Economic Cooperation
and Development and presents some of the unique approaches governments have taken to solve rural development problems.

622. Bickford, Deborah J., John M. Clapp, and Charles L.
      Vehorn. "An Econometric Analysis of Regional Employ-
      ment: Effects of Federal Economic Development Pro-
      grams." *Growth and Change* 17, no. 1 (1986): 1-16.
      Develops an econometric model in which marginal
effects of federal economic development programs for
different regions can be estimated. The authors review
past efforts in econometric modeling and point out where
their approach differs. Then, the model and data are
presented. The results indicate that lagged employment
effects from federal economic development assistance
were not strong for direct loans and loan guarantees;
however, economic development grants registered small
but significant lagged employment effects that differed
by both region and industry.

623. Brown, David L., and Kenneth L. Deavers. "Rural Change
      and the Rural Economic Policy Agenda for the 1980's."
      *Rural Economic Development in the 1980's: Preparing
      for the Future* (item 607), pp. 1-1 to 1-31.
      Reports that rural America has different problems and
opportunities in the 1980s than in previous decades.
These differences are relevant to public policy concerning rural economic development. The primary rural issue
has moved from revitalization in the 1970s to economic
dislocation and stress in the 1980s. The economic,
social, and demographic diversity among rural areas
indicates that programs tailored to particular types of
rural economies may be more effective than more general-
ized programs.

624. Browne, William P., and Don F. Hadwiger, eds. *Rural
      Policy Problems: Changing Dimensions*. Lexington,
      Mass.: Lexington Books, 1982. 251 pp.
      Is divided into five parts that examine general rural
problems, rural population changes, problems of local
governments, and specific policy problems. Specifically
discussed are communities and their relationships to
agrarian values, the rural poor, political values in
communities, the impact of inmigration on local government, administrative variations, land use, housing,
crime, education, and rural development.

625. Chase Econometric Associates, Inc. "Rural Impacts of
      Monetary Policy." *Agricultural Economics Research* 33,
      no. 4 (1981): 1-11.
      Uses a multiregional econometric model to evaluate the
      impacts of changes in monetary policy on economic
      development in metropolitan and nonmetropolitan parts of
      each of four Census regions (North Central, Northeast,
      South, and West). Results indicate that nonmetropolitan
      regions are generally less affected by changes in
      monetary policy than are metropolitan regions.

626. Choate, Pat. "A New Approach to Nonmetropolitan
      Development: National Sectoral Policies." *American
      Journal of Agricultural Economics* 62, no. 5 (1980):
      1016-20.
      Explores present economic and institutional cir-
      cumstances that are key to national economic revitaliza-
      tion, describes how national sectoral policies can be
      used to guide national economic revitalization, and
      assesses the development capacities of nonmetropolitan
      areas to participate in this process.

627. Clark, Marsha R.B. *The Contribution of Economic
      Development Agencies to Economic Growth and Revitali-
      zation in Seven States: Delaware, Maryland, North
      Carolina, Pennsylvania, South Carolina, Virginia, West
      Virginia.* Baltimore, Md.: The Johns Hopkins Univer-
      sity for Metropolitan Planning and Research, 1978.
      141 pp.
      Presents an economic portrait of seven states to
      demonstrate how development programs fit the historic,
      social, political, and economic conditions for which
      they were designed.

628. Cook, Edward A., and Marion T. Bentley. *Revitalizing
      the Small Town Mainstreet.* WREP 92. Corvallis, Ore.:
      Oregon State University, Western Rural Development
      Center, 1986. 11 pp.
      Describes the work of organizations and authors who
      have presented a relatively comprehensive program of
      downtown revitalization. Each program is described.
      The paper also summarizes relevant literature on the
      subject and focuses on the unique characteristics
      associated with downtown revitalization in small towns.

629. Cooke, Philip, and Gareth Rees. "The Industrial
      Restructuring of South Wales: The Career of a State-

Managed Region." *Policy Studies Journal* 10, no. 2
(1981): 284-96.
Examines the causes of the current economic crisis in
the industrial region of South Wales. The authors
contend that past and current government policies have
played a major role in bringing about the crisis by
contributing to the vulnerability of communities in the
area. Legislation is reviewed, and alternative strategies are critiqued.

630. Cornman, John M. "Prospects for Rural Development
Delivery Strategies and Programs in the 1980s."
American Journal of Agricultural Economics 62, no. 5
(1980); 1027-36.
Argues that what is needed is not an urban versus
rural development policy, but rather a national policy
with delivery strategies and programs appropriate to
urban or rural areas. Cornman discusses several
international, national, and rural issues that may
influence the development of such a policy.

631. Day, Theodore E., Hans R. Stoll, and Robert E. Whaley.
Taxes, Financial Policy, and Small Business. Lexington, Mass.: Lexington Books, 1985. 167 pp.
Provides empirical evidence on the differential impact
of federal taxation on small and large firms, discusses
the method and adequacy of financing small firms, and
compares the returns earned by investors in small versus
large publicly held firms.

632. Deavers, Kenneth L. "Social Science Contributions to
Rural Development Policy in the 1980s." *American
Journal of Agricultural Economics* 62, no. 5 (1980):
1021-26.
Examines the contributions of social science to
understanding the linkages between national issues and
trends, and rural economic and social conditions.
Deavers uses the energy industry as an example.

633. Dillman, B.L. "Rural Development in an Austere Environment: The Challenge of the Eighties." *Southern Journal
of Agricultural Economics* 14, no. 1 (1982): 55-64.
Discusses the challenges and opportunities created by
the Reagan administration's efforts to cut government
spending. Dillman elaborates on rural development
theory and practice and on the effects of the shift from
federal to other levels of spending.

634. Drabenstott, Mark, Mark Henry, and Lynn Gibson.   "The
      Rural Economic Policy Choice." *Economic Review
      (Federal Reserve Bank of Kansas City)* 72, no. 1
      (1987): 41-58.
      Points out that policymakers can choose between two
      rural policies: (1) a rural transition policy to
      facilitate and ease the costs of transferring people and
      resources to other sectors of the economy or (2) a rural
      development policy using public funds to subsidize
      economic development in rural areas. The authors
      outline the factors policymakers should weigh in
      choosing between the two policies and describe the
      elements that each might contain.

635. Drudy, P.J., ed. *Regional and Rural Development: Essays
      in Theory and Practice*. Chalfont St. Giles, Bucks,
      Great Britain: Alpha Academic, 1976. 117 pp.
      Examines the effectiveness of rural development
      policies in eliminating regional inequality in income,
      employment, infrastructure, and population growth in
      rural areas of Great Britain and France.

636. Dudley, Geoffrey. "The British Steel Corporation and
      Problems of Political Management." *Political Quarter-
      ly* 55 (October/December 1984): 427-37.
      Examines the 1982 decision by the British Secretary of
      State to continue operating all five major integrated
      sites of the British Steel Corporation (BSC). Tradi-
      tionally, the BSC had made the decision on particular
      plant closures and had recommended that a closure be
      made to achieve financial viability. Also examined is
      the increasingly active and interventionist role played
      by the EEC in shaping steel policy throughout the
      Community and the problems of implementing that policy.

637. Duncan, William A. "An Economic Development Strategy."
      Social Policy 16 (Spring 1986): 17-24.
      Reports that state and local economic development
      organizations are reorienting their strategies, with
      programs aimed primarily at attracting industrial branch
      plants being replaced by new emphases on fostering
      innovation and local initiative. However, the author
      contends that political strategies need to be integrated
      with investment-oriented projects in order to achieve
      the institutional changes needed to alter the distribu-
      tion of benefits and opportunities.

638. Farnham, Paul G. "The Targeting of Federal Aid:
      Continued Ambivalence." *Public Policy* 29, no. 1
      (1981): 75-92.
      Reports that, although there has been a trend toward
      the lessening of federal control over grant-in-aid
      programs, all affected groups have exhibited ambivalent
      attitudes on this question. The author illustrates the
      reasons for this ambivalence by examining both the
      process by which the U.S. Department of Housing and
      Urban Development categorical grants for urban and
      community development were transformed into the com-
      munity development block grant program and the debate
      that has occurred over the implementation and renewal of
      this legislation.

639. Findeis, Jill L., and Norman K. Whittlesey. "Trade-Offs
      in Resource Use: Implications For State Economic
      Development." *The Review of Regional Studies* 16, no.
      2 (1986): 50-57.
      Examines the extent to which irrigation development of
      approximately 800,000 acres in the Columbia River Basin
      stimulates secondary economic activity in Washington
      State. The analysis takes account of the competition
      between irrigation and hydropower generation in the
      Basin. The paper focuses on the distributional issues
      surrounding the expansion of irrigation and on a
      methodology for assessing such issues.

640. Flentje, H. Edward, ed. *Kansas Policy Choices: Report
      of the Special Commission on a Public Agenda for
      Kansas*. Lawrence, Kans.: University of Kansas Press,
      1986. 210 pp.
      Summarizes findings of special studies dealing with
      (1) the Kansas economy, (2) the future of rural com-
      munities, (3) state and local finance, (4) capital
      finance and public infrastructure, (5) educational
      governance and finance, and (6) preventive health care.
      Contains items 565, 595.

641. French, Julia R. *Education and Training for Middle-Aged
      and Older Workers: Policy Issues and Options*.
      Washington, D.C.: National Institute for Work and
      Learning, 1980. 48 pp.
      Examines education and training policy in view of the
      labor force implications of an aging U.S. population.
      French overviews the state of existing knowledge related
      to aging, education, labor force retention, and retire-
      ment; examines labor force disincentives in current

Social Security and private pension policies that
encourage older workers to retire and contrasts these
policies with the influences of the Age Discrimination
in Employment Act; discusses personnel implications of
an extended working life; and examines precedents in
human resource development that takes aging into
account.

642. Grindle, Merilee S. "Anticipating Failure: The Im-
      plementation of Rural Development Programs." *Public
      Policy* 29, no. 1 (1981): 51-74.
      Reports that integrated rural development programs are
      difficult to implement but that planners can anticipate
      major problems by directing attention to the decisions
      that most frequently cause problems. These tend to
      cluster at three points: when programs are defined,
      when specific delivery strategies are chosen, and when
      decisions about who is to get what at the delivery site
      are made. Implementation can be improved by altering
      either the content of the policy or its context at these
      three points.

643. Haas, Gregory. "Minnesota Star Cities: Lighting the
      Path of Economic Development." *Small Town* 16, no. 2
      (September-October 1985): 12-15.
      Outlines the Minnesota Star City program, which
      assists cities in developing a comprehensive economic
      development program by providing them with an effective,
      locally generated framework.

644. Hall, John Stuart, and Alvin H. Mushkatel. "Local
      Influence over National Policy: The Case of Community
      Development." *Public Policy Across States and
      Communities*. Edited by Dennis R. Judd. Greenwich,
      Conn.: JAI Press, Inc., 1985. pp. 75-90.
      Discusses the evolution of the Community Development
      Block Grant program, which has become both a major
      financial resource for American towns and cities and a
      principal instrument of national urban policy.

645. Hansen, Niles M., ed. *Growth Centers in Regional
      Economic Development*. New York: The Free Press, 1972.
      298 pp.
      Examines the benefits and problems of using the growth
      center strategy to promote economic activity that would
      presumably spill over into rural areas. Twelve authors
      discuss such topics as the general theory of polarized
      development, development poles, growth pole policy in

Canada and the United States, and employment growth and
change in unemployment at the county level.

646. Hayden, F. Gregory. "A Geobased National Agricultural
Policy For Rural Community Enhancement, Environmental
Vitality, and Income Stabilization." *Journal of
Economic Issues* 18, no. 1 (1984): 181-221.
Argues that past agricultural policies, dominated by
the interests of large agribusiness, have resulted in
adverse effects on rural communities and on the quality
of the environment. The author advocates policy changes
that would remove fragile land from production, restore
wetland and wildlife areas, encourage cost-cutting
organic farming, and promote diversification into
alternative crops and livestock enterprises. Many
current agricultural problems are viewed as stemming
from inappropriate agricultural technology; the author
emphasizes that a much more intensive effort to assess
the holistic consequences of agricultural technology
needs to be undertaken in the future.

647. Kuehn, John A., and Lloyd D. Bender. "Nonmetropolitan
Economic Bases and Their Policy Implications." *Growth
and Change* 16 (January 1985): 24-29.
Points out that rural areas are becoming more diverse
and reports a first step toward classifying nonmetropolitan counties into groups that have differing
characteristics related to policy objectives. The
classification is based on a county's type and mix of
basic economic activities, which in turn are believed to
influence the social and economic characteristics of the
people living there and their adjustments in response to
external economic events.

648. Kunde, James E., and Daniel E. Berry. "Restructuring
Local Economies Through Negotiated Investment Strategies." *Policy Studies Journal* 10, no. 2 (1981): 365-
79.
Examines the experimental process called the Negotiated Investment Strategy, which is a method for
coordinating federal, state, and local (public and
private) expenditures at the community level. The
method was tested in three cities: St. Paul, Minnesota;
Columbus, Ohio; and Gary, Indiana.

649. Liebschutz, S.F. "Community Development Dynamics:
National Goals and Local Priorities." *Environment and
Planning C: Government and Policy* 2 (1984): 295-305.

Reports that the dynamics of U.S. federalism has been the object of considerable scrutiny among scholars in recent years as federal aid to states and localities increased dramatically. Among the various forms of aid that emerged over the past decade were block grants designed to give greater autonomy to local decision makers. However, it is possible to undermine that goal by aggressive federal administration of the funds. Findings concerning program choices and beneficiaries show the exercise of considerable local autonomy at the same time that localities are responding to the preferences of the national government.

650. Long, Richard W. "Rural America: Perspective on Policy." *Public Administration Review* 46 (May/June 1986): 279-83.
    Discusses the problems of the 1980 Rural Development Policy Act and of trying to establish government programs or strategies on the basis of rural and urban differences. Long points out that rural regions are vulnerable to economic trends and the effects of macroeconomic policies because of the tendency of each to depend on a narrow economic base.

651. Luloff, A.E. *Rural People and Places: A Symposium on Typologies, Proceedings*. Pub. No. 47. University Park, Pa.: Pennsylvania State University, Northeast Regional Center For Rural Development, 1987. 213 pp.
    Reports on the papers and discussion of an assembly of researchers, extension personnel, government employees, and others interested in rural development policy creation. The volume contains twenty-one papers presented at the conference as well as summaries of three panel discussions.

652. Lynch, John E. *Local Economic Development after Military Base Closures*. New York: Praeger Publishers, 1970. 350 pp.
    Examines the economic impact on twelve local communities of the closure or inactivation of U.S. military installations and highlights the economic development strategies used by the communities in conjunction with the Office of Economic Adjustment (OEA). The study describes the activities and philosophy of the OEA and presents a blueprint for other communities that face similar circumstances.

653. Maclennan, Duncan, and John B. Parr, eds. *Regional Policy: Past Experience and New Directions*. Oxford, England: Martin Robertson & Co., 1979. 334 pp.
Traces the development of regional policy and changes in the nature of regional economic problems in Great Britain in the 1960s and 1970s, discusses neglected areas in formulating and implementing regional policy, and considers the future operation of regional policy under changing institutional conditions.

654. MacMillan, James A., and Shirley Lyon. *The Interlake Experience: A Description and Evaluation of a Rural Development Program*. Occ. Series No. 9. Winnipeg, Manitoba: University of Manitoba, Faculty of Agriculture, 1977. 176 pp.
Describes and evaluates a new approach to rural development in Canada. Initiated in the mid-1960s, the Fund for Rural Economic Development was an attempt to introduce two new approaches: (1) areawide planning, and (2) comprehensive, joint local, provincial, and federal programming including human capital stocks (manpower and education services, counseling, etc.), as well as public infrastructure (roads, schools, veterinary clinics, parks, industrial parks, etc). The rationale for these two new elements was that a focus on land use and resource productivity improvements for Canadian agriculture severely restricted the scope of the attack on the problems of geographical pockets of low rural income in Canada.

655. Nelson, Glenn L. "Elements of a Paradigm for Rural Development." *American Journal of Agricultural Economics* 66, no. 5 (1984): 694-700.
Addresses issues surrounding a paradigm for rural development by (1) developing the consequences of the lack of a generally accepted paradigm, (2) presenting a framework by focusing on target variables, policy instruments, and the structural relationships that link causal factors and target variables, and (3) drawing conclusions about developing better paradigms and improved policy analysis.

656. Nelson, James, and Luther Tweeten. "Systems Planning of Economic Development in Eastern Oklahoma." *American Journal of Agricultural Economics* 57 (1975): 480-89.
Develops a model that simulates the results of potential policy strategies directed toward alleviating problems of underdevelopment in rural areas. For each

strategy simulated, limited public funds are assumed
allocable among various types of development activities,
such as public assistance, human development, and job
development. Public assistance and industrialization
programs were found to be the necessary bases of
potentially successful development plans.

657. Ponting, J. Rick, and Nigel Waters. "The Impact of
      Public Policy on Locational Decision-Making By
      Industrial Firms." *Canadian Public Policy* 11, no. 4
      (1985): 731-44.
      Reports on a survey of the locational behavior of over
one hundred firms, which at some time during the period
1978-1983 had considered locating in the Canadian
prairie provinces. Included are firms that did and did
not decide to locate in this region. The results are
compared to other surveys carried out recently in
Alberta and the United States. The influence of
government incentive and disincentive policies at
various levels is generally found to be minimal. The
policy implications of the survey with respect to
environmental protection, transportation, the locational
search process, industrial linkages, and governmental
responses are considered.

658. Pulver, Glen C., and Glenn R. Rogers. 1986. "Changes
      in Income Sources in Rural America." *American Journal
      of Agricultural Economics* 68, no. 5 (1986): 1181-87.
      Outlines historic changes in the dependency of rural
America on farm and nonfarm sources of income. The
authors conclude that the economic revitalization of
rural America is dependent upon development and ac-
tualization of a comprehensive rural development policy.

659. Reid, J. Norman. "Development Strategies for Rural
      Areas." Paper presented to the Virginia Economic
      Developers Association, circa 1987. Available from
      the author at Room 324; 1301 New York Ave., N.W.,;
      Washington, D.C. 20005-4788.
      Reviews the principal program options available to
national, state, and local rural development policymakers in the current economic and political environment. Reid argues that, although developers have
historically emphasized attracting new firms and
retaining and expanding existing ones, local self-
development strategies that focus on new firm startups
should merit greater attention.

660. Ross, Peggy J., and Stuart A. Rosenfeld. "Human
     Resource Policies and Economic Development." *Rural
     Economic Development in the 1980's: Preparing for the
     Future* (item 607), pp. 15-1 to 15-25.
     Contends that the economic vitality of rural com-
     munities depends on the availability of a high-quality
     work force. The public investment in education and
     training programs has been substantial, but the alloca-
     tion of resources to rural areas is proportionally less
     than to urban areas. Furthermore, few programs address
     the unique needs of rural communities and rural people.
     Educational and training programs have made modest
     differences in the lives of rural residents, but they
     have not eliminated, nor even substantially reduced,
     poverty among rural families. To develop human resour-
     ces in rural areas, programs and policies need to meet
     the most pressing rural needs, including the alleviation
     of poverty.

661. Schmandt, Henry J., George D. Wendel, and George Otte.
     "CDBG: Continuity or Change?" *Publius: The Journal of
     Federalism* 13 (1983): 7-22.
     Questions the view that the folding of the categorical
     aids for urban revitalization into the community
     development block grant (CDBG) marks a sharp break with
     the past. The argument is made that this shift does not
     represent a basic revision of redevelopment policies and
     strategies on the part of either the federal government
     or the cities. The history of federal aid to local
     communities over the last several decades is charac-
     terized less by change than by continuity in program
     substance if not in form.

662. Smith, Michael Peter, Randy L. Ready, and Dennis R.
     Judd. "Capital Flight, Tax Incentives and the
     Marginalization of American States and Localities."
     Public Policy Across States and Communities. Edited
     by Dennis R. Judd. Greenwich Conn.: JAI Press, Inc.,
     1985. pp. 181-201.
     Points out that, because economic development is
     overwhelmingly important to localities and states, their
     political leaders are eager to obtain a larger share of
     national economic growth. They are handicapped,
     however, because states and localities have become
     marginalized actors within the federal system--meaning
     that they have been granted responsibility for the
     economic and social welfare of their citizens but have

neither the resources nor the political power to fulfill
their responsibilities.

663. Steinnes, Donald N. "Business Climate, Tax Incentives,
      and Regional Economic Development." *Growth and Change*
      15, no. 2 (1984): 38-47.
      Uses dynamic models, which explain the locational
      interrelationships between economic activities over
      time, to investigate what effect, if any, policy
      variables (tax incentives and interstate differences in
      tax rates) have on the locational decisions of economic
      entities. Using a time series approach, the author
      seeks to determine empirically if changes or differences
      in the policy variables have any influence on economic
      growth and development.

664. Sternlieb, George, and James W. Hughes, eds. *Revitaliz-
      ing the Northeast*. New Brunswick, N.J.: Rutgers
      University, Center for Urban Policy Research, 1978.
      443 pp.
      Examines the policy response to the economic changes
      in the Northeast United States. Specific topics include
      the new economic geography of America, a national policy
      toward regional change, making redevelopment politically
      acceptable, spatial inequity, job-creation incentives,
      taxation, the aging industrial legacy (labor force and
      wage rates), energy realities, capital supplies,
      welfare, and declining cities.

665. Summers, Gene F., and Frank Clemente. "Industrial
      Development, Income Distribution, and Public Policy."
      Rural Sociology 41, no. 2 (1976): 248-68.
      Examines the public policy implications of industrial
      development and its effects on the income status of weak
      competitors in a community system. Age, sex, education,
      and labor force status were regarded as resources that
      indicate the competitive capacity of individuals.
      Changes in the parameters of a causal model that relates
      competitive capacity and income were estimated using
      longitudinal data from rural Illinois regions.

666. Sweet, Morris L. *Industrial Location Policy for
      Economic Revitalization: National and International
      Perspectives*. New York: Praeger Publishers, 1981.
      184 pp.
      Discusses (1) governmental policies and programs that
      directly or indirectly control the locational pattern of

industry, (2) policy effects on industrial development, and (3) industrial policy. Included under direct controls are those in the United States, Great Britain, and Western Europe, as well as locational controls on foreign direct investment. Discussed under indirect controls are codetermination and plant-closing legislation.

667. Taylor, Nick, Mike Abrahamson, and Tracy Williams. *Rural Change: Issues for Social Research, Social Assessment, and Integrated Rural Policy.* Canterbury, New Zealand: University of Canterbury and Lincoln College, Centre for Resource Management, 1987. 32 pp.
   Draws ideas together from several years of research and social assessment work by students and staff at the Centre for Resource Management on aspects of rural social change. The expanding New Zealand and overseas literature on rural sociology, social science in resource management, and social impact assessment of rural change is added to this review to provide indications of current trends in the social structure of agriculture, and to identify some areas for further applied social research.

668. Tweeten, Luther. "Enhancing Economic Opportunity." *Communities Left Behind: Alternatives for Development* (item 224), pp. 91-107.
   Sets forth a comprehensive program for enhancing economic opportunity in communities and areas characterized by population decline or stability. Several important issues are discussed: (1) increasing the quantity of local resources versus using existing resources more efficiently, (2) resolving local problems by action of the community itself versus action at the multicounty or national level, (3) the dilemma of equity versus efficiency in development programs, and (4) whether to emphasize place or people prosperity in development programs.

669. Tweeten, Luther. "New Policies to Take Advantage of Opportunities for Agricultural and Rural Development." *Interdependencies of Agriculture and Rural Communities in the Twenty-first Century: The North Central Region* (item 269), pp. 215-26.
   Reviews rural development opportunities and problems and suggests an appropriate federal response.

670. Wilkinson, Kenneth P.   "Implementing a National Strategy
      of Rural Development." *The Rural Sociologist* 4, no. 5
      (1984): 348-53.
         Suggests directions for future federal efforts toward
      improving the well-being of residents of small towns and
      rural areas.

Indexes

Author Index

Subject Index